Praise for Dragonflame

"The spiritual imagery of **Dragonflame** is markedly hybrid—a unique admixture of philosophy, magic, folklore, and metaphysics. Through innovative and carefully calibrated rituals, exercises, and other devotional practices, Leo offers readers profound tools of personal transformation. **Dragonflame** is thus a book that radically empowers its readers to seek new heights."

—Marlene Hennessy, PhD

"This magical guide to meditation is deeply spiritual and purposefully eclectic. **Dragonflame** is creatively executed and brilliantly written in a style that will win the hearts of the novice and adept alike. Leo has found a way to gracefully marry psychology and the universal language of the psyche."

—Marie DeFeo, Psy.D., Licensed Clinical/Forensic Psychologist

"Expect the unexpected from this stylish and magical self-help book. A series of guided meditations includes reflections on astrology, Qabalah, alchemy, and the tarot. Each chapter brings the reader more deeply into self-awareness."

—Claudia Carpenter, manager of New Age Books & Things, Ft. Lauderdale, Florida

"**Dragonflame** resists any attempt to be described in simple terms. It is at once a grimoire and a guide for self-empowerment. Its heart is a series of meditations. They include ritual magic, astrology, and the tarot, all of which lead the reader on the most important of journeys: the journey within. A must-read!"

—Domenic Leo, PhD, author of *Images, Texts, and Marginalia in a 'Vows of the Peacock' Manuscript*

DRAGONFLAME

DRAGONFLAME

Tap Into Your Reservoir of Power Using Talismans, Manifestation, and Visualization

LAWREN LEO

New Page Books
A division of The Career Press, Inc.
Pompton Plains, N.J.

DRAGONFLAME
EDITED AND TYPESET BY KARA KUMPEL
Cover design by theBookDesigners
Printed in the U.S.A.

To order this title, please call toll-free 1-800-CAREER-1 (NJ and Canada: 201-848-0310) to order using VISA or MasterCard, or for further infor-mation on books from Career Press.

The Career Press, Inc.
220 West Parkway, Unit 12
Pompton Plains, NJ 07444
www.careerpress.com
www.newpagebooks.com

Library of Congress Cataloging-in-Publication Data

Leo, Lawren
    Dragonflame : tap into your reservoir of power using talismans, manifestation, and visualization / by Lawren Leo.
        pages cm
    Includes bibliographical references and index.
    ISBN 978-1-60163-310-1 -- ISBN 978-1-60163-477-1 (ebook) 1. Magic. I. Title.

BF1612.L445 2014
133.4'3--dc23

                                                                        2013045965

This book is dedicated to
all those who are searching for the key
that will open the door
to their true destiny.

ACKNOWLEDGMENTS

My thanks and love go to my siblings, niece, parents, and my cousin Leonard Greco, whose constant love and support became the backbone of this book.

My heartfelt thanks go to my mentors, some alive and some passed: "Mother" Mary Glomb, Angie Costanza, and Anne R. Capdeville. I also thank my dear friend and confidante Linda Mazzocca for her trust and unwavering confidence in me.

My deep appreciation goes to all my friends, students, and especially my muses (you know who you are)—may you continue inspiring authors as they cross your paths.

Congratulations and deep thanks to Nathaniel Dailey for his spectacular illustrations.

CONTENTS

A NOTE FROM THE AUTHOR

DANCING AROUND THE FIRE

If we are to wield great magic, then let us learn from great teachers: the alchemists—magicians par excellence. Their goal, known as the Great Work, was to find the Philosopher's Stone: a magical substance capable of turning lead into gold. They understood that "lead" and "gold" were symbols for states of being, such as "lack of knowledge" and "enlightenment," respectively, as well as actual metals. This allowed their ultimate motivation to be self-transformation, not greed.

When humanity was still young, the secrets of alchemy were hidden in symbols and made practically undecipherable for the novice in order to protect the transformative powers from being abused or absorbed by an unprepared psyche. But we are no longer living in the Middle Ages, and from one generation to the next, Earth's technology is becoming more and more advanced, demanding spiritual sophistication in order to balance the scales of evolution. In this book, I offer a solution: a simple, yet powerful philosophy that uses the principles of alchemy. I call it Dragonflame.

In these pages you will learn how to awaken potent magical forces lying dormant within you through the energies of the Lion, Horse, and Unicorn totems. The mixture of these three totems is the crux of Dragonflame. Its sacred fire turns metaphorical lead into gold and is the embodiment of an ancient magical philosophy made anew.

All your goals can be obtained through magic as long as your purpose is pure and ultimately aimed at self-transformation—this is the true meaning of the Philosopher's Stone (hereafter called the Stone). Magic is fire. This book teaches you how to dance around it, enjoy it, and respect it without getting burned.

The Dragonflame name and concept were brought to me by Spirit through two-and-a-half decades of astral experiences, lucid dreams, psychic epiphanies, readings, and spirit communications. I now share it with you through both simple and complex creative visualizations, spiritual exercises, spells, and rituals. In this way, you can practice and eventually master these techniques and witness an amazing effect: the realization of your purpose and the discovery of your dream—and how to create it!

Dragonflame

INTRODUCTION

WHAT DRAGON IS THIS?

Someone once told me that if you can see yourself doing what you want in your mind, then you can do it in real life. Some years later, I came to understand that statement as one of the hermetic axioms: "as above, so below." Another way of saying it is this: If you can visualize a goal strongly enough in your mind, then it will manifest on the earth plane in one way or another—but it has to be done correctly. It must be a complete formula utilizing the following ingredients: Goal, Purpose, and Sacrifice. Otherwise the magic will not work. *Dragonflame* is the instruction manual that will teach you how to follow the complete formula successfully.

Buried deep within each one of us lies a treasure. It is our mission in this lifetime to find this treasure, but its exact location is known only by the dragon that guards it. Ready and willing to guide you to your true destiny, the dragon waits only for you to call. This dragon has been known by many names throughout the ages: the Philosopher's Stone (the Stone), the Triple Goddess, kundalini, chi, the Green Man, and IAO (Isis, Apophis, Osiris) are just a few. It is the embodiment of a magical philosophy of birth, death, and rebirth, or goal, sacrifice, and purpose. Harnessing this power is the key to continued success in all avenues of your life. I have simplified this magical philosophy through a talisman I have named Dragonflame. Understanding the Dragonflame gives you a new and powerful way to work magic to achieve deep spiritual transformation and to manifest your desires in a karmically correct fashion.

The dragon I am introducing you to is a holy and regal creature; it is an aspect of Nature already residing within you. Its parts are very much like those of a horse or unicorn, making it tame enough to ride. Think how much easier it would be to traverse your inner landscapes on the back of such a potent force, using its power to know yourself and expand your consciousness. Learning its parts is the first step to calling forth its magic.

Dragonflame's anatomy comprises three main parts: a unicorn's horn, a horse's body, and a lion's tail. For each part, you will find a corresponding chapter in this book (Chapters 1–3) containing four sections and four exercises, visualizations, or rituals, as follows:

- ✳ Philosophical explanation and matching exercise
- ✳ Astrological explanation and matching exercise
- ✳ Tarot association and matching exercise

✳ Alchemical explanation and matching exercise

Chapters 1, 2, and 3 focus on three of the 12 astrological signs and their corresponding elements: Virgo/Earth, Scorpio/Water, and Leo/Fire. (I have purposely left out the remaining nine in order to simplify an otherwise complex magical formula.) Dragonflame's core element is fire. Although the element of air is taken into consideration, where the concepts of transformation and transmutation are concerned, the element of fire almost always takes center stage.

There is also a section called Enhancements for the Advanced Student at the end of certain exercises, with helpful information for the serious student or aspiring magician. Most of the information in the Enhancements sections focuses on the moon phases and the Qabalistic Tree of Life, a contemporary form of the Hebraic tradition outlining the creation of the universe on both a microcosmic (visible) and macrocosmic (invisible) level. It is designed as a reference to guide the advanced student in further studies and research.

In order to fully utilize Dragonflame's potential, take your time following the exercises for each chapter and do not proceed with the next exercise until you feel confident that you have mastered the one before it.

Once you understand Dragonflame's anatomy, your training becomes more involved. Chapter 4 will help deepen your connection with Dragonflame's energies by activating them through initiation and by teaching you how to make and consecrate a Dragonflame talisman. You will be led through several meditations and thought-provoking questions to deepen your relationship with Dragonflame and help your subconscious mind become more attuned to its vibratory level.

All magicians must follow a karmic or moral code. Chapter 5 will briefly discuss these rules and the proper treatment of spirits/forces encountered in the next chapter's rituals, including the magic circle and how to create it, preparing your altar, blessing and extinguishing candles, and how to thank and release the spirits.

Chapter 6 is aptly titled "Rituals of Transformation." I have organized the rituals based on Sephiroth (see the Glossary) four through ten. (I have not left out the first three, for it is with the Supernal Triangle that we "work" the rituals and aspire to our soul's highest aspiration.) Each ritual demands the utmost attention and respect. The rituals have been designed on a particular level of difficulty to impart the far-reaching consequences each will yield if done properly. *Transformation* entails having the courage to look at life's tribulations as spiritual tests. I have chosen seven specific rituals and gods/goddesses that will test your magical stamina and call on your courage. Whichever ritual you choose, Dragonflame's philosophy will help you follow through successfully and ground harmonious energies.

A main theme throughout the Dragonflame philosophy is the use of sacrifice: letting go of something lesser in order to obtain something greater (see Chapter 2 for more on this). I have improvised on this concept with the idea of user-friendly sacrifices to be practiced on consecutive days. I call them Willpower Lists, and they are a fantastic way to raise power for any ritual or spell. Once you grasp the concept, it is easy to create your own, but until then, an Appendix at the end of this book can help stimulate your creativity.

Tools You Will Need

Before beginning *Dragonflame*, you will need several magical tools: any deck of tarot cards (as long as it is a standard 78-card deck), a blank journal to log your experiences and measure progress, and an incense holder or oil diffuser (whichever you prefer). The blank journal (hereafter called the magic journal) is of special importance.

Dragonflame's rituals and exercises are designed to help enrich psychic creativity—your inner landscape of insight and imagination. Psychic creativity is much like artistic creativity. It starts in the soul and mind and can be cultivated through inspiration, study, and hands-on practice. The only difference is that instead of the painter's canvas, the magician uses the magic journal to convey or record feelings and experiences. Taking time to write your thoughts, experiences, and innermost feelings in a magic journal will help stimulate your dreams and allow you to better understand your unconscious mind. As time passes, you may notice recurring symbols or images in your entries that have been trying to speak to you or relay a message. Also, the results of a particular ritual may manifest months, even years after it has been performed. The magic journal gives you the opportunity to go back to the original date it was performed, record the result, and analyze it further. In this way, your magic journal becomes a private diary holding all your psychic thoughts, and will prove to be a source of inspiration and knowledge through time. It will become a personal grimoire of magical and spiritual evolution that may be handed down to future generations, or kept hidden, as you see fit.

Various other magical supplies will be necessary for the exercises and rituals in this book and will be listed under

Enhancements in Chapters 1–3 and under Supplies and Offerings in Chapter 6. All tools and most supplies can be easily purchased at your local metaphysical store or via the Internet.

It is also necessary to procure an altar in order to work Dragonflame's magic properly. An altar can be permanent or temporary, round or square. It can be as simple as an upside-down cardboard box covered with a tablecloth, or as elaborate as an antique oak cabinet with a granite top. The key word here is *practicality*. All that matters is that you hold your altar in reverence as a sacred space and understand its esoteric meaning (see The Altar: As Above, So Below on page 123). Traditionally, altars are set up facing either North or East. I suggest facing your altar toward the East, where the sun rises, symbolizing white magic, resurrection, and spirituality.

Power is the energy that makes magic work. It is the universal life force. You tap into this magical force the way you use electricity—by plugging into it and allowing its current to run through you to your goal. Similar to electricity, it is neutral. However, if misused deliberately or unwittingly, it is potentially harmful. You are a conduit, and in order to direct the current properly, you must be clean and well-insulated, so to speak. Drug and alcohol abuse, or any unhealthy addiction, will interfere with the magical process and impede spiritual development.

A final note to send you on your way: A reservoir of power is waiting for you. Even if you live in a hut and have only enough money to put food on the table, you can still work magic. Everything you need to begin lies inside your heart, mind, and soul.

Use the Dragonflame philosophy to take up the reins of destiny and embrace your personal journey of creativity, spirituality, and magic!

The Hermit's Lantern, Virgo, the Unicorn's
Horn, and Alchemical Mercury

CHAPTER 1

UNICORN'S HORN— PURPOSE

Philosophical Explanation

The Unicorn's horn on Dragonflame represents purpose—where all things magical start and end. Purpose is the underlying reason or motivating factor for our goals, and is an essential ingredient for materializing a thought successfully. If the goal is what you want to achieve, then the purpose is why you want to achieve it. Without purpose, reaching your goal will have little or no meaning.

Dragonflame's horn closely resembles a unicorn's horn for two important philosophical reasons: (1) in medieval times the unicorn's horn was believed to have the ability to neutralize all poisons; and (2) only a maiden of pure virtue (a virgin) could attract or tame the unicorn.

In magic, these reasons translate into a key lesson: if your purpose is pure, then your karma will be too. What good is it to wish for success, yet deep down feel that you do not deserve it? Perhaps you were taught that money is the root of all evil or that the amount of success you receive will only be equal to the amount that you suffer. This is poison fed to us by man-made belief systems. The unicorn's horn teaches us how to neutralize the poison of negative thoughts and emotions by analyzing our purpose and keeping it pure like the maiden.

For instance, if your goal is continued success with the purpose of having peace of mind, then you have made a conscious decision to use your money to create peaceful conditions. This is very different from simply stating that you have a goal of achieving success—that equation is not complete. The proper purpose creates a positive and solid vision that will be accepted by the conscious mind as well as the subconscious mind. It completes the equation that equals acceptance on all levels. The motivational force works for you even while you are unaware or asleep. It is in constant motion, and, once you have aligned it with purpose, it will not be blocked or sabotaged by the poison or fear that has been programmed into your core. But how do you do this? How do you align your will with a purpose?

The following is a simple awareness exercise to help get you on your way. It is a natural method designed to create awareness of your trains of thought, making it easier for you to learn how to observe them. There is also a wonderful side effect to this exercise—astral travel and/or lucid dreams. The astral realm is a state of being that exists beyond the third dimension. The physical body has adapted to the Earth's three-dimensional realm. It vibrates at a denser state, creating flesh, bones, and material items navigated by the five physical senses. The sixth sense, however, is not bound to the third dimension. It exists to help us navigate and communicate with the astral realm via thoughts, feelings, intuition, and the astral body, thus giving us more control over the physical realm. Just as the physical body vibrates at a slow, dense state to match the Earth's vibrational frequency, the astral body vibrates at a higher, subtler one, in tune with the astral realm's frequency.

The astral realm seems to be a limitless place of exploration—a multidimensional realm, unfolding worlds within worlds, individually created for each person's destiny, likes, and dislikes. The astral realm has been called the collective unconscious, or the ethers, and can also be considered layers of our psychic nature discernable by the psyche and astral body. Entering this realm has also been called lucid dreaming.

A lucid dream is one in which you become aware that you are dreaming. Suddenly becoming conscious that you are flying is a common example of a lucid dream. It is another form of astral travel and can be triggered by the following awareness exercise. The more you use the awareness exercise, the more it will help your astral body transfer the memory of its experience to your brain upon its return to your physical body. In turn, you will begin to recall your dreams in more detail, stimulate lucid dreaming (becoming aware that you are dreaming), and even create a spontaneous astral experience (waking up, or becoming lucid, on the astral plane).

The phrases "as above, so below" and "all change begins within" can be translated to mean "all change begins with thought, on the astral plane or within a lucid dream, before it begins to manifest on the Earth's third dimension." It is a magical key and is best cultivated slowly. Be patient with yourself and practice the awareness exercise as often as possible. Have your magic journal handy to jot down thoughts and experiences at the end of the exercise.

AWARENESS EXERCISE

becoming the observer: (finding purpose)

One way to think of the unicorn horn is as universal love. In this way, it corresponds with the heart chakra, one of the main psychic centers in which we find purpose. (A chakra, meaning "wheel" in Sanskrit, is a connection point between the physical body and the spiritual realm, or one of many energy centers found on the body.) Every so often throughout the day, stop and focus your will on your heart chakra (located between the breasts in the center of the chest). Remind yourself to become aware that your heart is beating, constantly circulating blood and oxygen to keep you alive. A trigger to help remind you of that thought could be turning a light on or off.

Now take it a step further. When this thought enters your mind, become aware of whatever tasks you are performing and ask yourself why you have chosen to perform them. Ask the question as many times as you need to until you find a positive purpose. If you can find no positive purpose, assign one to the action. For example, I wake up from a night's sleep, walk into the kitchen, and turn the light on. This action brings about a moment of awareness in me. My train of thought goes something like this:

*I have just turned a light on...I choose to bring aware-
ness to my heart chakra...my heart is beating, keeping me
alive...there is purpose behind all of my actions, no matter
how great or small... What am I doing at this moment?
Making coffee... Why am I making coffee? To help wake myself up...because I enjoy the taste...the sound of coffee brew-
ing and the smell make me happy.*

My train of thought is clear and positive. I am
making coffee (the goal) because it makes me happy (the purpose). Here is an example of a task that
needs to be assigned a positive purpose:

*I have just turned a light on...I choose to bring aware-
ness to my heart chakra...my heart is beating, keeping me
alive...there is purpose behind all of my actions, no matter
how great or small... What am I doing at this moment?
Washing dishes... Why am I washing the dishes? So they will
be clean...because no one else is going to wash them...because
there will be a mess if I don't clean them...because I do it
by habit...it's unhygienic to leave them dirty...once they're
clean, I can move on to more important things...*

In this example, my train of thought is not entirely positive. So, in the end, I choose to assign this
positive purpose to the goal of cleaning the dishes:
*Because I feel that I have accomplished something, and it
brings a small sense of peace.*

Try this particular exercise at least twice a day.
Through consistent practice, you will be implement-
ing a type of self-discipline that will always end on
a positive note. As you gain skill at becoming more
aware of your thoughts, you will become more

proficient in the art of isolating goals and defining their purpose in your life.

One of the keys to successful magic is becoming aware that the consequences of your actions can be controlled through purpose. The unicorn's horn is a symbol of connecting our thoughts with the Divine and inspiring our mind with higher purpose. Its philosophy, through this awareness exercise, will aid mental acuity and train the mind to have power over impulse-based goals by neutralizing them through strategy.

Astrological Explanation:
The Magic of Virgo

The astrological sign of Virgo governs the unicorn's horn, and rightly so. Virgo, meaning "virgin" in Latin, reminds us of purity of intent and conjures images of the famous 15th-century tapestry *Lady with the Unicorn,* found in the Cluny Museum in Paris.

In magical philosophy, the maiden is an aspect of the Triple Goddess symbolizing birth or new beginnings. She represents a new foundation or birthing place for your idea. The birthing place is the purpose. The idea is the goal. This is better understood through Virgo's element, earth.

Think of purpose as the concave space in the earth that the gardener digs to receive and protect his seed, or goal. This is the beginning of creation; the way you will begin to create—with purpose. The unicorn's horn reminds us that purpose creates fertile soil in which to plant our seed. Even the spirals of the unicorn's horn make us think of the Goddess and her spiral dance of creation.

VISUALIZATION EXERCISE

MYSTERY OF CREATION: (FINDING A WAY TO PURSUE YOUR DREAMS)

The Egyptian goddess Isis has been worshipped for more than 5,000 years as a symbol of fertility. In fact, one of her titles is Lady of Green Crops, alluding to rich vegetation and bountiful harvests. The astrological sign Virgo is also associated with Isis. One of Virgo's main stars, Spica, was visible in Egypt during the wheat-harvesting season, and Virgo is associated with the element of earth, one of nature's birthplaces. In this guided visualization, you will use her energies to find your own patch of land and make it fertile. In this way, you will be telling your subconscious mind to prepare an area to spring forth new life. This new life can be whatever you choose. It can be whatever your dream is, or even the realization that a dream exists. In this exercise, you are taking the first step in finding a way to pursue your dreams, even if you do not know what those dreams are yet.

To begin, find a comfortable place to sit or lie down. Make sure you will not be bothered for at least 15 to 30 minutes, and do not forget to put your cell phone on silent. Take a few slow, rhythmic, deep breaths through your nose, exhaling through your mouth. Mentally tell yourself to relax. Let go of the worries of the day. Forget about the past and the future. All that exists is the present moment. Now, begin your visualization (you may want to record yourself reading the visualization first and play it back so you can keep your eyes closed):

Imagine an untouched piece of land far away from any buildings. The grass is short and the earth is soft, ready to be gardened. No man-made structure has ever been built on this piece of land. It is a perfect, sunny day without a cloud in sight. Breathe in the smell of the earth. Sense its strength and life beneath your feet. You see the goddess Isis seated before you on the ground in lotus position, wearing a long, white and blue tunic, the colors of heaven and wisdom. Her hair is long, black, luminous. She bends her torso towards the ground, thrusts her hands into the soil, and speaks the word "fertility." The tone of her voice is gentle, but her controlled authority makes her blessing final. It vibrates into the earth and through your entire being. You feel peaceful, understanding your limitless potential. Isis has hollowed out a portion of the earth for you: a shallow safe haven prepared to receive and nurture your seed to full blossom.

You may stay in that vision as long as you like. When you are ready, open your eyes and record any experiences and/or feelings you had in your magic journal. Allow yourself to be aware of your inner potential to do or be anything you want every time you see or think of the earth. This *awareness* takes us inward as we look outward and can activate a spontaneous illumination or feeling of brilliance.

Enhancements for the Advanced Student

* On the Qabalistic Tree of Life, the colors white, blue, and black (queen scale) are associated with the Sephiroth Kether, Chesed, and Malkuth, respectively. Do some extra homework and look up these Sephiroth to deepen the meaning of your visualization. Remember, knowledge is power.

* Take a bath in lavender oil just before your visualization and/or burn lavender incense. You can also light a green candle to Isis to represent fertility (you may either extinguish the candle with a candle snuffer or let it burn out naturally).

* Perform on the new moon, on a Friday, or when the moon is in Virgo.

Tarot Association: The Hermit and His Lantern

The tarot card of the Hermit is associated with Virgo and therefore with the unicorn's horn. The Hermit's message is to go within, just as he goes within his cave to receive a message from his higher power. He has no fear that the cave is dark because his lantern burns brightly. The unicorn's horn is the same as the hermit's lantern.

Just as the hermit's lantern safely contains fire, so does the unicorn's horn safely contain the very essence of Nature. The unicorn's horn illuminates, or sheds light, on the path you are walking, giving you the ability to see ahead. This inner fire held within the horn is associated with the Hebrew letter Yod (י). *Yod* translates into English as "hand" or "open hand," and is the 10th letter in the Hebrew alphabet. Within the hermetic Qabalah (see page 135 for more on this) Yod is believed to be the spark of life, the birthplace of nature. The unicorn's horn is the home for this divine spark, which is also known as purpose.

Purpose creates a belief in a higher power, directing you toward your goal on the best path possible. The purpose contained in the unicorn's horn brings to light negative emotions and thoughts, thus enabling us to confront them. Once we confront a fear, we gain control over it, and, consequently, grow more powerful.

magical exercise

my decision is final: (contracting with yourself)

The purpose of this exercise is to help you find and confront your fears. It is a simple, yet profound way to change your life.

From a standard 78-card tarot deck, take out Major Arcana IX, the Hermit, and place it on your altar (see page 123 for more on this). The Hermit presides over this ritual to remind you that the only obstacles blocking you from finding purpose and fulfilling your dreams are your fears. By performing this rite, you have now decided to become like the Hermit and pick up your lantern to dispel the darkness and confront your fears.

At the top of a clean page in your magic journal draw the Hebrew letter Yod (׳). Beneath it, write the decision to confront your fears in your own words. It can be as long or as short as you want. All that matters is that you mean it. You are materializing your thoughts on the earth realm by writing them and therefore creating a contract with yourself.

When you are finished, sign and date it. At the bottom of the sheet write, *With harm to none and for the greatest good of all. So be it.*

Leave it on your altar or somewhere safe for three nights.

Here's an example of one I did:

׳

With all the power in me and with all my heart and soul I now decide to confront my fears consistently. I am larger than my fears and have control of them. I am light, I am truth, I am courage.

[sign and date]

With harm to none and for the greatest good of all. So be it.

Enhancements for the Advanced Student

* Use a sheet of parchment paper. Write with a stylus and Dragon's Blood ink.

* Perform on a new moon.

* Perform when the moon is in Libra.

* Light a yellow candle to represent light and illumination (you may either extinguish the candle with a candle snuffer or let it burn out naturally).

* Do some inner homework and write down your fears and worries. Defining them is the first step in confronting and purging them.

Alchemical Explanation: The Alchemy of Enlightenment

The unicorn's horn is also associated with alchemical mercury. Alchemy is, in the simplest terms, the act of speeding up evolution. It is intended to refine our subtle body by transmuting one vibrational level of our being to a higher vibrational level. This process is known as the Great Work, and it happens automatically when we have a purpose, goal, and sacrifice—the embodiment of the Dragonflame philosophy. Without these three concepts, magic will not work. They are the rules of the universe, and they are spearheaded by the unicorn's horn, purpose.

The unicorn's horn holds the spiritual essence of alchemical mercury, which allows Dragonflame to communicate with the entirety of its parts. Through its philosophy, it teaches us how to reach our Higher Self and receive enlightenment. This happens naturally when a goal is aligned with a purpose.

Alchemical mercury gets its name from the Roman god Mercury, the messenger of the gods. Communication is one of this god's major talents. The Roman poet Ovid wrote of Mercury carrying Morpheus's dreams from the valley of Somnus to sleeping people. We are going to borrow the idea behind this myth and ask Mercury to carry a message to our Higher Self as we drift off to sleep, as described in the following magical exercise.

magical exercise
1 get the message: (discovery of enlightenment)

Enlightenment happens when you are *in the light* of your interior spiritual sun. The god Mercury, acting as a go-between, will help connect you with this source of light. He can place your foot on a new path illuminated from within, the path that leads to fulfilling your destiny and completing the Great Work.

The Petition

To begin, light a blue candle to the god Mercury. Using your finger, put some essential oil of orange on your brow, throat, and solar plexus (a small amount is all you need). Say,

Great god Mercury, bring my message directly to my Higher Self so I may discover my true will. Thank you in advance.

As you fall asleep, repeat this request over and over: *Show me where I need to go and take me there.*

Do this for three nights in a row. Use your magic journal to jot down any thoughts or dreams that come to you. The idea behind this exercise is to get the petition directly to your subconscious mind during alpha state. Alpha state occurs just as you begin to fall asleep when your mind is in a semi-trance. This is the state that a hypnotist will shoot for when trying to relax a client to receive positive affirmations.

Enhancements for the Advanced Student

* Perform on a new moon.
* Perform on a Sunday.
* Read about the Sephirah Hod on the Qabalistic Tree of Life.

Summary

This chapter introduced you to the first part of the magical philosophy I call Dragonflame. It embodies three concepts: goal, purpose, and sacrifice. Without these three components, your magic will not work. Each concept, represented by a totem, can be found on Dragonflame's anatomy: the lion's tail (goal), the unicorn's horn (purpose), and the horse's body (sacrifice). In order to understand the power behind Dragonflame, you must first start with the unicorn's horn and what it represents: purpose.

The concept of purpose lies hidden just beneath the surface of every goal. Dragonflame's philosophy teaches us to tap more deeply into the power of purpose through each of the magical associations attributed to the unicorn's horn:

* **Astrological sign Virgo (August 23–September 22).** Virgo teaches the mystery of creation, which starts in our mind. The organizational skills of this earth sign help us learn to observe our train of thoughts, to sharpen self-discipline and self-awareness, and to cultivate a positive attitude.

* **The Egyptian goddess Isis.** Although any goddess representing fertility or motherhood may be associated with the unicorn's horn, I have chosen the Egyptian goddess Isis. An integral player in the myth of Osiris's death and resurrection, her name has been invoked and worshipped for thousands of years. Her power quickly evokes mystical feelings, as Isis is a well-known archetype in the collective consciousness of humanity—ideal wife, mother, sister, and magician.

* **Tarot Card Major Arcana IX, the Hermit; the Hebrew Letter Yod.** By following the Hermit into his cave and discovering the power behind the Hebrew letter Yod (ʼ), we come to understand that purpose creates a belief in a Higher Power, directing you toward your goal on the best path possible. The purpose contained in the unicorn's horn brings to light negative emotions and thoughts, thus enabling us to confront them. Once we confront a fear, we gain control over it, and, consequently, grow more powerful.

✳ **Alchemical mercury.** Aligning a goal with a purpose helps us achieve spiritual enlightenment through the concept of alchemical mercury. Through the principle of alchemy, we learn that the unicorn's horn is the essence that allows all of Dragonflame's components to communicate properly with one another, and its language is that of purpose.

Each of the magical, visualization, and awareness exercises throughout this chapter is designed to introduce new information to your brain on a conscious and subconscious level. Through practice, a new philosophy as taught by Dragonflame will begin to form on the highest level of the Divine. This process is known as the Great Work, and it leads to the Stone.

Scorpio, Sickle, the Body of a
Horse, Alchemical Salt

CHAPTER 2

HORSE'S BODY— SACRIFICE

Philosophical Explanation

Imagine that there is a mountain before you. The mountain is your purpose. Reaching the top is your goal. The arduous yet rewarding journey to the top is your sacrifice. Dragonflame gets you up there, and its body, which is that of a horse, does it most efficiently.

The horse represents the four concepts of magic: to will, to dare, to know, to be silent. Collectively, these disciplines create a potent energy called sacrifice. To clarify, the sacrifice I am speaking of within this book is self-sacrifice and has nothing to do with shedding blood or harming yourself or anyone else.

For a thought to manifest on the earth realm, a sacrifice must occur. Think about this for a moment: A goal originates from a vision, a thought. No matter what your goal is, once you start taking steps to solidify that thought, you have made the decision to let go of something lesser in order to obtain something greater—the very definition of sacrifice.

Let's use a career as an example: Your vision is to be self-employed and have financial security. In order to obtain this you *must* work extra hours and spend more time concentrating on and being at the business and less time at home. By doing so, you have already sacrificed being at home, hobbies, or any other pleasant things you may have been doing other than working. Most important, you have also sacrificed one of the greatest commodities known to humankind: time.

Often, the drive to reach our desired outcome is so strong that what we sacrifice to get there becomes an accepted reflex of the subconscious mind. In other words, we are not aware of our sacrifices because our mind is set on achieving the goal. "Ambition can be blinding"—isn't that how the saying goes? And, in the long run, this can cause regrets, which can be perceived as suffering. Creating your goal without acknowledging sacrifice will hinder and even stop your progress. It would be like walking up the mountain instead of riding horseback.

Conscious use of sacrifice ends suffering through awareness and acceptance. Let's take a quick look at our career example again from this perspective: Your vision is to own your own business and have financial security. In order to obtain this you *choose* to work extra hours.

Notice that by changing one word, from *must* to *choose*, you have changed your entire frame of mind. That's it. It is that simple a concept—awareness of choice. Just being aware of and consciously choosing the sacrifice allows you to accept it. At the end of the day, all that matters is how we have chosen to spend our time. By becoming aware of the choice, you have begun manipulating time with an incredible power: your will!

mαgicαL exeRcise: το wiLL
(poweR means progress: you are only αs good as your word)

Power can be defined or gauged in many ways. In magic, one way is through progress. The stronger your will becomes, the more adept you become at directing its force toward your wish or desire. Moving toward this wish or goal is considered progress.

The following practice is used in magic to discipline and sharpen your will. It teaches you how to create energy to direct toward any goal through conscious sacrifice. Its premise lies in choosing different tasks, one for each day of the week, and completing them successfully. If you say you will do it, then it will be done. To emphasize this point, you will start each sacrifice with the words *I choose*. Here is a sample willpower list using the goal and purpose of this magical exercise—to sharpen your will (goal) so that you may increase your magical power (purpose):

Monday: *I choose* to meditate on a positive trait that I would like to foster.

Tuesday: *I choose* to not drink coffee for 24 hours.*

Wednesday: *I choose* to refrain from text messaging for 24 hours.

Thursday: *I choose* to abstain from using profane language.

Friday: *I choose* to visit a deceased relative or friend's gravesite.

Saturday: *I choose* to create peace by not engaging in any arguments.

Sunday: *I choose* to dedicate at least one hour to my magical studies.

*All Willpower Lists are based on a 24-hour day. In other words, if you choose to abstain from drinking coffee, it would be from midnight to 11:59 p.m.

Do not sacrifice something because you think it is morally wrong or a bad habit. Simply do it because you say so. Remember, the objective is to hone your will through awareness, not to suffer. Do not judge your sacrifices—they are all neutral! And, if you say you are going to clean the bathroom cabinet on Wednesday, then clean it on Wednesday, not Tuesday or Thursday. It does not work like that: the sacrifice has to be done on the allotted day for your will to be strengthened. If you break the continuity of your list, get up, brush yourself off, and start over.

You are only limited by your creativity when it comes to putting together a Willpower List, so put some original thought into it. If you smoke cigarettes, try stopping for three days. Or dedicate one day to taking the children somewhere fun or donating your time to a nonprofit organization. The list can start on any day you like and run for as short or as long amount of time as you like. I recommend seven days to start.

Now it's your turn. Write your own seven-day Willpower List to sharpen your will (goal) so that you may increase your magical power (purpose). Write the list on a separate sheet of paper, not directly into your magic journal, as you will need to burn it after the ritual is finished.

Once you have your list together, place it on your altar with the tarot card Ace of Wands.

The Ace of Wands represents your will and is associated with the element of fire. By placing it on the altar, you are telling the universe that you have chosen to increase your magical power. You are telling the universe that you are aware that sacrifice creates psychic energy and that you want guidance in directing its force.

Each day, check off your completed task. On the last day, burn your list completely and blow the ashes to the wind while saying,

Great Goddess, I humbly offer you this energy. Open my heart to your knowledge.

With harm to none and for the greatest good of all. So be it. Thank you in advance.

Enhancements for the Advanced Student

* You can work a Willpower List for any length of time. Following the rhythm of the moon phases makes it stronger. To initiate, complete, or jump-start projects, work a cycle during the waxing moon—new moon to the full moon. To remove obstacles or hindrances, work a cycle in the opposite direction during the waning moon—full moon to new moon.

* Light a purple candle to represent power (you may either extinguish the candle with a candle snuffer or let it burn out naturally).

* Vibrate the God name Shaddai El Chai (see page 133 for more on vibrating God names) nine times a day for the duration of your willpower list, beginning as soon as you wake in the morning. Feel it vibrate through your entire body as you pronounce each word.

* Look up the Sephiroth Yesod and Geburah on the Qabalistic Tree of Life.

* Research the tattwa for fire, Tejas.

Astrological Explanation: Scorpio's Potion

The horse's body is associated with the astrological sign of Scorpio. There is much to gain from this intense sign of the zodiac, known to be one of the most daring. Scorpio's power supplies the food that keeps the horse aspect of Dragonflame in motion. Two key "food sources" are determination and courage.

Determination is a fixed purpose or intention. Through the power of determination, you create a fixed course straight to the target, your goal. When you are determined to see something work or to follow through on a project, you have created a new mindset. Your perspective becomes anchored on victory and very little can stop you. This is the energy we are looking for to reach our goals, the energy we want to be able to conjure in order to give us that edge above the rest. Scorpio's energy gives us the power to pursue our desire with keen force. But it is not enough on its own. We need its complementary color, so to speak—courage.

Courage can mean "without fear" or "the opposite of fear." This is the energy needed to initiate yourself into the mysteries. When this happens, you start to learn about yourself, and a true inward journey begins, filled with adventure and magical expansion. Courage is what enables us to work through the "fight-or-flight" syndrome in difficult situations and evolve as humans. It helps us deal with stress and become leaders, not followers.

The more you feed Dragonflame courage and determination, the more fears you will conquer, the more control you will gain, and the more powerful you will become. If you are going to use a potent energy, however, you must use it with respect, for Scorpio's dark side can be as lethal as its poison. Fear, jealousy, anger, worry, resentment, and doubt are just some of the emotional poisons found under Scorpio's negative aspect. They are in each and every one of us at one time or another, and they must be defined so they can then be banished. In order to use Scorpionic determination and courage successfully, you must first gain permission from the god that presides over Scorpio, Hades.

Hades, Greek god of the underworld, was believed to judge the souls of humans and decide whether they went to Tartarus (Christian equivalent of hell) or the Elysian Fields (Christian equivalent of heaven). He represents that aspect in ourselves that guards the correct way out of a personal labyrinth of darkness and onto the path of the mysteries. He judges our worthiness to gain access based on our purpose.

VISUALIZATION EXERCISE: TO DARE

(SCORPIO'S POTION: COURAGE AND DETERMINATION)

This meditation asks you to set out boldly to obtain Scorpio's potion—courage and determination. To do so, you must face Hades with a true purpose, if you dare. Will you be sent to Tartarus or the Elysian Fields?

To begin, mix the following essential oils in an oil diffuser and place it on your altar as an offering to Hades: three drops of cypress, four drops of thyme, and three drops of allspice. (I put water in the diffuser's receptacle and then add the oil. Putting the oil directly onto the receptacle may damage it and causes too much smoke.)

Next, find a comfortable place to sit or lie down and follow the relaxation instructions from Unicorn's Horn, Magic of Virgo on page 33.

Begin your visualization:

You are standing in an underground labyrinth. All about you is darkness. The stone floor beneath you is cold, and the air is heavy and musty. You put your arms out to either side (forming a T shape with your body) to see how wide the chamber is, and find you can place each palm of your hand against the walls. Just as a surge of fear arises you rebuke it by moving onward. You will not allow yourself to be overcome. You sense the walkway is becoming narrower, but there is no way you are going back. The path you left behind has nothing to offer, no secure place to put your feet. All that counts is this moment, present tense. You decide that you will find the path that leads to what you are meant to do in this lifetime no matter what. And then your eyes deceive you, or so you think. The darkness moves as if alive. Adrenaline pumps through your veins. "Take a deep breath," you tell yourself. Relax, blink, breathe, look again. You catch a glimmer of something gold. A quick, tiny spark in the midst of the blackness. You look more closely You are trying to make out its shape, round maybe...yes, round rings. Leaning forward to touch them, you feel an ache in your gut. Something is wrong; you can sense it. Darkness moves again, maybe a foot or so in front of you. Your heart is beating rapidly now and you are having a hard time swallowing from the anxiety. Just when you think you will die, two huge eyes appear in the darkness. And finally, you make out the full image—a man, enormous, seated on a monolithic throne. You are gripped by fear. His body is covered with black hair. He has the head of a bull and a gold ring through his septum. He smells of musk, like a wild animal. Without a word spoken, you understand that he is asking what it is you seek. Unable to respond at first, your body is taken over by a higher force. You sense you are trying to point your right forefinger to the ceiling as if to say, "Up there, that is where my purpose is, toward the light." Telepathically, you hear him respond, "You must know darkness in order to know light." You blink your eyes and he is gone. Thankful for this blessing, you breathe a sigh of relief. If you had been in his presence for one more second, surely you would have perished from fear. You were pushed to your very limit. Now you are on the surface of the earth and it is daytime. In front of you is an altar; behind the altar is a long path. Your right hand is still pointing up toward the sky. Now point your left hand down toward the earth, proclaiming a magical principle: "As above, so below." On the altar are the building blocks of creation: fire, water, air, and earth, and inside of you is Scorpio's potion—courage and determination. Now you can feel it. Now you can use it.

Open your eyes. Log any experiences in your magic journal.

Enhancements for the Advanced Student

* Light a black candle to represent burning away fears and negativity (you may either extinguish the candle with a candle snuffer or let it burn out naturally).

* Research the myth of the Minotaur.

* Research Apophis, Greek god of darkness. This deity represents a dark stage or dark night of the soul that one goes through just before an epiphany or rebirth. He represents the death or decomposition that

> symbolically happens just before an evolved
> energy emerges. Replace Hades with Apophis
> in the above meditation.
>
> ❋ Research the tattwa for water, apas.
>
> ❋ Perform on the night of the dark moon and/
> or Saturday, the day of Saturn.

Tarot Association: Death and His Horse

The tarot card Death (or Major Arcana XIII) and Nun, the Hebrew letter found on it, are both associated with the horse's body. One thing we know for sure is that death exists. At one point, our physical vehicle must die, and thus our energy will change form. With the understanding of this concept, our lives change, and what we would like to accomplish in this incarnation takes on new meaning. The importance of change and the acceptance of change start moving to the forefront of our thoughts.

Major Arcana XIII teaches us that for change to occur, there must be a death of some sort. This is nature's law. One of the most powerful changes is the death of an old, useless belief or pattern so a new and evolved one may spring up in its place. This can be very painful and usually happens naturally after some kind of tragedy occurs, forcing us to look inward for answers. But we have the power to change voluntarily, and there is something wonderful and awe-inspiring about that power. Because change creates opportunity, when we do it through purpose and awareness, we are working with the fates, and in turn they smile upon us. In order to achieve a particular goal, we must learn to change voluntarily. Knowledge is the key to making this happen.

A simple example would be changing careers. Perhaps you are a waiter or waitress who aspires to become a nurse. Going to school and obtaining knowledge will allow you to shed the skin of working in a restaurant and embark on a new career. A more in-depth example would be quitting smoking cigarettes. A logical first step might be finding as much information as possible on addictions, nicotine, and negative thought patterns. By educating yourself, you begin to remove helpless feelings. The second step might be self-analysis, or interviewing yourself. Why do you like smoking? What do you associate with smoking? What part of your personality or ego is the smoker? After this knowledge is digested and mixed with your natural desire to quit smoking, a conscious internal change can occur. This may come through a lucid dream or a sudden feeling of awareness. The healing takes place when you become aware that smoking is a part of your ego that you no longer want, a part of the old you that you do not need anymore and can willingly leave behind. This may sound complex, but the message is simple: knowledge plus application of knowledge equals change.

In magic, knowledge, thoughts, and the realm of the mind are associated with the element of air. It is all around us, but it cannot be seen. We survive by breathing it in and extracting oxygen molecules from it. Believe it or not, this process of osmosis is found within the tarot card Death through Nun, the Hebrew letter associated with it.

Nun, the fourteenth letter in the Hebrew alphabet, translates as "fish." A fish, not being aware of itself, has no idea that it is able to survive under the water due to osmosis, but we have something special—our intellect, which can create something I like to call *conscious osmosis*: the slow and steady accumulation of knowledge and affirmations.

Conscious osmosis allows us to bridle our passions, symbolized by Dragonflame's horse's body. Only then do we have the capability of directing its tremendous force. This also follows the iconological theme of Major Arcana XIII where some versions depict an image of Death seated on a bridled horse.

VISUALIZATION EXERCISE: TO KNOW

(CONSCIOUS OSMOSIS: ELEVATE YOUR MIND)

This meditation uses conscious osmosis to control the horse's body. It will teach you how to discipline and elevate your mind by using affirmations and creative visualization. This is a powerful way to obtain focus and should be practiced for at least one week out of every month.

To begin, each of the following affirmations is to be analyzed. For instance, the second affirmation uses the word *body*. I know I have a physical, an astral, a psychic, and a magical body. Your reality may be different. Ask yourself how many bodies you have. Do you believe this because of what you have read, or do you know this because of experience?

Look into this further and repeat the process of analysis with each affirmation. Question each word and what each affirmation means to you. When you are satisfied, move on to the next step. Along with each affirmation I have attached a brief analysis to help you get started:

1	**Affirmation:** Now I choose to be happy. **Analysis:** My emotional state is a choice. I do not have to be sad or suffer. Really, it is a choice to progress because I accomplish more when I am happy.
2	**Affirmation:** Now I choose to have control over my body. **Analysis:** This is to give more control over my body or collective bodies—spiritual, astral, and physical. *Control* connotes the ability to direct. Strong will. This helps with concentration, efficacy, intelligence, and a better flow of energy.
3	**Affirmation:** Now I choose to remember and understand all of my lucid dreams and astral travels clearly and accurately. **Analysis:** Part of my learning experience is in the astral and dream states; therefore, it is important to train myself to remember them as clearly as possible. Plus, I must understand them, or what use are they? This choice/affirmation will motivate me to analyze them as well as honor them properly.

4	**Affirmation:** Now I choose to face the present. **Analysis:** This means that I am able to see the past and future as well. By choosing to face the present, I am focusing on what is before me and not on creating anxiety. It means to face the problems at hand and not to run from them. It reminds me that my future is built on how I choose to deal with my present.
5	**Affirmation:** Now I choose to listen to my Higher Self. **Analysis:** To me, the Higher Self is that aspect of all knowing and wisdom that resides within each one of us. It exists because I choose to listen to it and therefore grant it credence. "I choose to be wise" would be another way to say this affirmation.
6	**Affirmation:** Now I choose to be a temple of light. **Analysis:** This is my inner temple. I follow a path of light. I draw illumination to my Self. I seek illumination.

7	**Affirmation:** Now I choose to be well balanced. **Analysis:** This affirmation means that I wish to balance all the elements that reside in me. If I am ill, this affirmation will bring me health on all levels. To me, this is choosing good health and life.
8	**Affirmation:** Now I choose to connect with my psychic consciousness. **Analysis:** This connects me with my psychic awareness. This affirmation is complemented by Affirmation #2. I can control my psychic body by connecting with it, and vice versa. This implies obtaining something beyond physical sensory experiences. Becoming more than human. It also implies using your psychic ability consistently and naturally during a state of normal consciousness.

Once you have finished your own analyses, the affirmations will hold more power. Each one is to be repeated three times and sealed with the phrase *so be it* every day for seven days. For example: *Now I choose to be well balanced. Now I choose to be well balanced. Now I choose to be well balanced. So be it!*

In total, you will repeat eight affirmations, three times each, every day for seven days in a row. On the eighth day, your release day, do not say your affirmations. Instead, go into a relaxed state and follow this guided meditation:

Imagine you are seated in a yoga or lotus position. You are hovering about three feet above a river that is flowing towards the ocean. The water is dark, but placid, and you are not afraid. Trees hang over the edges, obscuring the banks. Visualize yourself as perfect and beautiful, happy and extremely calm. You silently command yourself four times, "Up, up, up, up!" A beautiful wind is created by your momentum as you move ever faster forward and upward on a steady incline. This path leads to the fulfillment of your goals and the realization of your true identity. You lift your arms up to form a Y and feel a balmy wind against your palms. Breathe it into your being and imagine it as light blue. Begin collecting it. Feel its force and power. It is balancing you on your journey. Slowly, bring your hands over your chest in an X position, right over left, pulling all you have collected into your heart chakra. You are an ethereal being, a ray of light. There is no fear and there are no obstacles before you, just a bright, clear, open path. You are an extension of light. Now imagine that you have surpassed the speed of light. That law no longer applies. You have arrived at the essence of your soul, your true identity. Become aware of the outline of your body sitting in yoga position. Within this outline, your interior is filled with hypnagogic colors moving and vibrating slowly to the rhythm of the universe. Feel your navel area and solar plexus move and react to the vibrations of your voice as you intone the God name, Shaddai El Chai (sha - die' - el - hi). This name means the Almighty Living God *in Hebrew. Know that your inner strength has been quickened, reborn.*

All the knowledge that you have collected has been deposited within your navel chakra. You feel powerful. Finally, you have begun to understand the saying engraved upon a column at Delphi: "Know thyself."

Open your eyes. Log your experiences in your magic journal.

Enhancements for the Advanced Student

* ✳ Add to the list of affirmations or replace them with your own.

* ✳ Obtain a light-blue candle and draw a circle on it with the point of a quartz crystal. Light the candle and put the crystal in front of it before you do your affirmations. You may either extinguish the candle with a candle snuffer or let it burn out naturally when you are finished with your affirmations.

* ✳ Bless your brow chakra with essential oil of horehound prior to using the affirmations or meditation. This oil is associated with the energy of Mercury and enhances concentration and communication.

* ✳ Begin the affirmation process eight days before the full moon so that your release day falls on the evening of the full moon. Perform the meditation on the night of the full moon.

* ✳ Research the number 8 and its correspondence to Mercury on the Qabalistic Tree of life. Also, read about the Sephirah Hod.

* Research the correspondences of the moon and the Sephirah Yesod on the Qabalistic Tree of Life to help you better understand the element of air.

* Research the tattwa for air, vayu.

Alchemical Explanation: The Alchemy of Surrender

The horse aspect of Dragonflame corresponds to alchemical salt. Alchemical salt represents the protective covering around the soul or essence of matter. By better understanding the meaning of alchemical salt, we are able to go within our own protective covering where the magical elixir of the dragon lies. This is achieved through introspection and purification, or by practicing the art of silence.

Introspection means to look inward. In order to do this properly, you need to be quiet. Being quiet, which sounds deceptively easy, is one of the most difficult tasks or sacrifices in magic. There is an art to learning what you can and cannot share with others. This is also known as the gift of discernment, which leads to wisdom.

Once you have chosen a goal or idea to manifest, it becomes magnetized by your thoughts. By keeping the goal a secret, you keep it safe from others casting doubt or negativity onto it either purposely or accidentally. This is so important in the world of magic because even the slightest bit of doubt can distort or negate your wish from being born into the material realm, and here is where alchemical salt comes in to play.

Through alchemical salt's receptivity, it will attract your thoughts or vibrations and ground them properly. In fact, its element is necessary to bring your goal to life on the earth plane. It has deep protective qualities through concealment, just as keeping your goal hidden through silence protects it from the eyes of the enemy. It is also used for purification. This is easier to understand as a comparison:

Alchemical salt is a mixture of two elements: water and earth. What more natural a combination could you think of to cleanse yourself with than a natural spring pouring forth from a hillside? Or, when mineral (salt) becomes rock (earth). Once again Mother Earth provides the perfect example of purification if we think of a time when rocks and water were used to clean garments. When we apply these concepts to cleaning our inner selves, the spring water becomes a metaphor for cleansing our emotions and the rocks and garments become metaphors for purifying our egos, as garments often define who we are or would like to be in society.

The following exercise is designed to help you surrender to your Higher Self. Its journey will help you purify your inner self by releasing doubts and suffering into the physical element of salt. This will help you trust yourself more so you find it easier to know what information you need to share and what information you need to keep silent. It will also help release the energy that you have built up during a ritual and allow it to work for you through natural events that would otherwise seem like coincidences. Think of it as the winding-down aspect of magic.

visualization exercise: to be silent

(alchemy of surrender: Learning discernment)

Enter a relaxed state (see page 33) and begin the following guided meditation.

Imagine that you are falling through an abyss on your back. Feel the wind created by the momentum of your fall flowing upward around the outline of your body. Instead of becoming frightened, you choose to go with the feeling and see where it takes you. With this decision, you notice a change. You begin a backward somersault in mid air. You are now free-falling on your belly as a parachuter does when he/she first jumps out of an airplane. The feeling is invigorating as you transition from the abyss and into the earth's atmosphere. You have a calm, peaceful feeling as you enter the night sky and begin to make a slow spiral widdershins (counterclockwise) with perfect control. You hear yourself say,

I relinquish to my Higher Self. Grant me the wisdom to know what to release and what to keep silent.

With each circular layer, you funnel closer and closer to the earth until you make contact barefoot. The earth beneath the soles of your feet is soft and moist, the perfect mixture of soil and water. Not too hard, not too soft. You continue walking in a counterclockwise motion to the exact center of the funnel. Before coming to a standstill, you become aware of your physical body.

Open your eyes. Log your experiences in your magic journal.

Enhancements for the Advanced Student

* Become aware of what you say to others throughout the course of one day and night. Did you say too much? Too little? Try this once a week for one month.

* Perform on the new moon.

* Burn a white candle and essential oil of eucalyptus in a diffuser on your altar to Mother Earth as an offering prior to performing the meditation (you may either extinguish the candle with a candle snuffer or let it burn out naturally). Or place a bowl with some dried eucalyptus leaves on the altar to Mother Earth.

* Research the tattwa for earth, prithivi.

Summary

This chapter described the concept of sacrifice in detail, an important part of Dragonflame's magical philosophy. Represented by the body of a horse on Dragonflame's anatomy, sacrifice creates a tremendous flow of energy that can be harnessed through four magical principals: to will, to dare, to know, and to be silent. Each discipline is applied through the magical associations attributed to the horse's body:

* **Astrological Sign Scorpio (October 23–November 22).** The magical exercise in this chapter, "To Will," explains how to create and utilize a Willpower List to increase your magical power. We transform our lives

with promises—a vow to diet, to remain loyal, to remain sober. Sharpening our willpower and training our thoughts helps us tap into its ancient currents of intent and change. To make a promise is to wield magic, and it begins through proper use of our actions and deeds. Two positive attributes of the astrological sign Scorpio are used to feed Dragonflame's philosophy: determination and courage. Using them wisely, however, involves confronting Scorpio's negative attributes of fear and doubt, as symbolized by Hades, the Greek god of the underworld.

✳ **Hades, Greek God of the Underworld.** The magical concept of "to dare" is awakened in the psyche by confronting Hades. The guided visualization in this chapter brings you to Hades' lair. During this guided meditation, a self-initiation will occur as you are safely led through a dark labyrinth and into the light. Understanding that we have a dark side, exposing ourselves to it properly, and emerging from it safely are steps we must take in order to work with the principle of sacrifice and the magical concept "to dare." Any god or goddess of death or destruction may be associated with the horse's body as found on Dragonflame. The Egyptian god of darkness, Set (also known as Apophis in the Greek pantheon), is another good choice as he plays an integral part in the myth of Osiris's death and resurrection.

✳ **Tarot Card Major Arcana XIII, Death.** The idea of change lies behind the meaning of the tarot card Death. Change can either be voluntary or involuntary, controlled or left to chance. The Dragonflame philosophy combines the power of affirmation and the magical concept "to know" to help create conscious change.

✳ **The Hebrew Letter Nun.** The Hebrew letter Nun, associated with the Death card in the tarot, translates as "fish." A fish is unaware of itself. Using this concept, I have created an exercise to introduce the idea of conscious osmosis: the slow and steady accumulation of knowledge and affirmations. Conscious osmosis allows us to bridle our passions, symbolized by the horse's body on Dragonflame.

✳ **Alchemical Salt.** The equine aspect of Dragonflame also corresponds to alchemical salt. Alchemical salt represents the protective covering around the soul or essence of matter. Introspection and purification lead to a better understanding of the concept of alchemical salt. As we learn to go inward and meditate, the magical idea of how "to be silent" is achieved.

The concept of sacrifice and the four magical principles (to will, to dare, to know, and to be silent) incorporated into Dragonflame are symbolized by the horse's body and are the backbone of magic. Through the use of Willpower Lists, affirmations, and conscious osmosis, you will gain more control of your destiny and come one step closer to knowing your true will. The Dragonflame philosophy allows us to use sacrifice as a tool to sharpen the will and grow more powerful. It also explains that this takes place through proper use of courage, determination, and introspection.

Leo, Alchemical Sulfur, the Tail of a Lion, the Sun

CHAPTER 3

LION'S TAIL— GOAL

Philosophical Explanation

Dragonflame's tail is that of a lion; it represents your desires or goals. Having a goal creates a target to aim your will toward on the astral realm and enables you to cast magic safely and successfully. Most magic fails when it has to rely on poorly formed goals. This can be caused by lack of detail, description, or, more likely, desire. You have to be sure that the goal you choose is really what will make you happy. But how do you determine what goal will truly make you happy?

Sometimes answering the age-old question *What do I really want?* can seem outside of our grasp. But it isn't. The answer lies within our sacred space or universe; we just have to recognize what it looks like and begin our search. Understanding the mechanics of what makes a goal click will help shed some light.

Creating a goal is a lot like sailing a ship: We choose our destination and map out the best course possible. The ship is a metaphor for our thinking vessel, or conscious mind. It allows us to control and tap in to the energy of our thoughts and have safe passage over the sea, or our subconscious mind. As our only choice is to be the captain, it will be our knowledge of the art of sailing the vessel, or training our thoughts through the Dragonflame philosophy, that will help ensure arrival to our destination. Clearly stated, a goal is a destination.

One meaning for *destination* is the purpose for which something is destined. Within this simple definition lie two important mysteries. One, when we set a goal we are fulfilling our destiny. Even if we do not reach it, we have changed our lives and the lives of others by attempting to reach it. And two, it is our purpose that motivates our goal into action.

Understanding the navigational equipment will increase our knowledge and help us control our course. Ultimately, it comes down to what I like to call an easy-to-use Magical GPS system: **G**oal, **P**urpose, **S**acrifice. These are the only three abstract items you need in order for magic to work. As you've learned, put them together and they make Dragonflame.

Some of the great frontiersmen of the past used the Dragonflame philosophy naturally, including 15th-century Italian explorer Christopher Columbus. His goal was to find a fast maritime trade route to the East Indies. Instead, he landed in the Americas and became one of the first Europeans to establish settlements for Spain in the Dominican Republic and Haiti. It does not matter that he was not able to meet his intended goal. What matters is that he set a goal, believed it could be reached, and tried to obtain it. In trying to live his dream, destiny met him half way. Columbus taught us something invaluable: Take a risk, explore new horizons, and you may find your dream. He was a true adventurer...and magician too. Whether he knew it or not.

Magical Exercise
(Explore Yourself Further: Find Your Dream)

Become a magician; realize your dream. Take up the reins and ride Dragonflame across the horizon and discover what is on the other side.

For this exercise you will need one violet or light purple candle, essential oil of gardenia (to dress the candle), essential oil of orange (to use in the oil diffuser as an offering), and three tarot cards—Major Arcana I (the Magician), the Nine of Cups, and the Ace of Wands.

God or Goddess: Mercury, Ancient Roman god of communication

Duration: Seven days starting on any new moon

To begin, place the three tarot cards on your altar in the shape of a triangle.

Placement	Tarot Card	Meaning
Top of triangle	Major Arcana I, the Magician	Purpose. Where your dream is located.
Lower left	Nine of Cups	Your dream or desire. What you love.
Lower right	Ace of Wands	Your will or sacrifice. What you are willing to give up in order to achieve your dream.

Center the cards and candle on your altar. Place the offering in the upper left corner:

Candle

Major Arcana I

Nine of Cups   Ace of Wands

Orange
Offering

The three points on a triangle can correspond to Dragonflame's personality—fire, power, and transmutation as well as purpose, goal, and sacrifice. Dragonflame's personality is the outcome or byproduct of working magic properly, allowing you to receive good karma and experience spiritual transformation.

Next, dress the candle with the following goal and purpose using essential oil of gardenia:

Goal: Explore myself further

Purpose: So that I may find my dream

Sacrifice: Make a Willpower List and follow it for seven days minimum. One of the days must be to go somewhere new, even if it is a park in a neighboring town.

(Helpful Note: When I performed this exercise, I used a waxing moon phase. My Willpower List started on the new moon and ended on the full moon. I chose to do something each day that made me happy. For instance, reading something new, taking an aromatherapy bath (by mixing Epsom salt and essential oil of lavender together and placing 1/2 to 1 cup under running bathwater), walking outside, listening to music, dancing, or eating something I love. Also, I focused my attention on something new, such as listening to jazz and learning some of the artists' names.)

Every day, for the duration of the ritual, put eight drops of 100-percent essential orange oil in an oil diffuser and light it as an offering to the god Mercury. It is Mercury who will enable you to locate your dream by communicating with your Higher Self, either consciously or subconsciously.

Each day or night light the candle and enter a relaxed state (see page 33). Concentrate on the following guided visualization.

Walking out the door of your home, the thought to go somewhere entirely new unexpectedly arises. It's a balmy, bright day. Gentle breezes seem to raise your spirits as the landscape around you changes into an immense, lush field, a sea of perfect green grass bending in the wind. In front of you is what appears to be a unicorn standing underneath the only tree in sight. Catching each other's eyes, you make a telepathic connection. You receive a message from the creature in a stream of thought:

I am a magical creature called Dragonflame. I am a part of you, hidden until this very moment. My essence is ruled by transmutation and fire. To understand me is to understand destiny. To ride on my back is to wake from a primordial sleep.

You are on its back now and surprisingly not frightened at all. Holding on to the reins and feeling secure in the saddle, you head off into the field with Dragonflame. Sensing your desire to go somewhere new, Dragonflame heads toward the mountains. But there are two paths to take.

As soon as you question which is the correct path, a beautiful melody sings through you. It is carried by the wind. The melody is perfectly to your liking. In fact, the thought crosses your mind that if you had to write a song, it would sound exactly like this one. You decide to follow the music to its source. Dragonflame speaks:

What you are hearing is your dream calling out to you. It summons you forth. Your dream has a will too. All you need to do is match its frequency and you will find one another directly. Think of your dream as a person meditating on the goal of meeting you. You share the same wish—to find one another. When you realize this, you are closer to realizing your dream.

The curious tune mesmerizes you more fully as you climb to the highlands and reach a level plane. There, in the openness of the prairie next to a running brook, you are surprised to see a lone cabin. Leaving Dragonflame by the water, you almost float toward the humble home. The front door is open, as if to indicate you do not need permission to enter. You pass through its archway and directly to one of the bedrooms. There, in this bedroom, is an androgynous youth lying in meditation. As you stand next to the bed, the youth awakes and sits up shocked to see that his or her own magic to draw you forth has worked! You join hands in happiness—your right hand with the youth's right, your left hand with the youth's left. Together, you have created an infinity symbol.

For so long you have wondered, Where does my wish lie? *Now you know. There is overwhelming happiness shared between the two of you. You will always remember the exact location of this cabin, and you may visit as often as you like to communicate with one another.*

Open your eyes. Log any experiences in your magic journal.

Enhancements for the Advanced Student

* Begin the ritual on the new moon in the planetary hour of Mercury.

* End the ritual on the full moon in the planetary hour of Jupiter.

* Perform the LBRP (Lesser Banishing Ritual of the Pentagram) and BRH (Banishing Ritual of the Hexagram) before beginning (see Glossary page 231). (A good explanation of the LBRP and BRH can be found in Donald Michael Kraig's book *Modern Magick*. See Recommended Reading section page 243.)

Astrological Explanation: Leo's Creativity

The lion's tail on Dragonflame corresponds to the astrological sign of Leo. This fiery sign supplies three key ingredients to successful goal-making: strength, confidence, and creativity.

Strength gives us the ability to follow through with a thought. If used consciously during the creation process, it increases patience and redirects misguided energy. This misguided energy may manifest as feeling overly worried or concerned about competition, income, love, or any aspect of living that wastes Leo's strength, which could otherwise be used for personal achievement.

On the road to personal achievement, we find many important decisions. They can either be made with doubt or with confidence. When we are confident in our decisions, we become natural leaders. The lesson here is that a confident decision makes a lasting goal.

The last ingredient, creativity, is a byproduct found from using original thought. But where is an original thought born? Originality is the last domino to fall in a chain reaction that looks something like this: inspiration moves an emotion, which moves a desire to express what we are feeling, which creates a thought. Sometimes this domino effect happens accidentally, and sometimes we have to seek it out. Taking a walk in the woods or listening to music are a few examples of how we can catch an inspiration and start a domino effect. A breathtaking act of nature like a lightning storm, a Zen-like sport, or an experience such as surfing can also kickstart a domino effect. So can falling in love.

The wonderful thing about original thoughts is that they are natural expanders. They expand your intelligence by forcing you to think beyond your normal mental limitations, and they take you deeper into your creativity, becoming additional colors on your soul's palette. Ultimately, they expand your horizons.

MAGICAL EXERCISE

Leo's Creativity: (Original Thought)

The ancient Greeks prayed to one of the nine muses, Clio, for inspiration. In the following exercise, you will call on her guidance as you focus on catching an original thought. For this exercise, you will need one sunflower-yellow candle (any size), essential oils of cinnamon (to dress the candle) and hyacinth (to use as an offering). You may also use olive oil.

God/Goddess: Clio

Duration: 1 day

Goal: Original thought

Purpose: Expand your horizons

Sacrifice: Burn some Hyacinth incense or oil as an offering to Clio. Olive oil also makes a wonderful oblation. Just put some in a bowl and place it on your altar for Clio.

To begin, dress the candle with cinnamon oil. Cinnamon oil is used for concentration and also corresponds to the elements of fire and air. Place it on the center of your altar. You can perform this exercise either standing or sitting. Once you choose, enter a relaxed state.

Next, light the candle when the big hand on the clock is going upward. For example, 9:35, 10:35, and so on. This symbolizes the big hand bringing the wish to you. As you light the candle, say:

Clio, daughter of wisdom, bring me inspiration from out of the blue.

Now imagine yourself sitting in the lotus position and floating mid-air in a blue sky. There is not a cloud in sight. Inhale to a slow count of 3 and say to yourself, "original." Hold the breath for a count of 3 while imagining the blue of the sky. Exhale to a slow count of 3, and say to yourself, "thought." Hold the exhale to a slow count of 3 while imagining the blue of the sky. Do this two more times. Breathe naturally.

Become aware of how your chest and abdomen move with each inhale and exhale.

Commit the following chant to memory, and repeat it out loud or to yourself in a rhythmic manner while focusing on the candle's flame:

Strength, Confidence,

Original Thought

I Seek You Out

Until You're Caught

When you feel satisfied, close your eyes and imagine a flaming gold image of the zodiac sign Leo in your mind's eye. This symbolizes that you have caught what you were seeking and solidifies the inspiration. Do this for a minute or two only.

You are finished. Let the candle burn out naturally. Thank Clio and the kind spirits for their help. If you used an oblation of olive oil, pour it outside, symbolically giving it back to the earth. Log any experiences in your magic journal.

Enhancements for the Advanced Student

* Begin the exercise on the new moon.

* Perform when the moon is in Leo (first choice) or Aquarius (second choice).

* During the chant, every so often, walk by your candle and visualize the zodiacal sign of Leo in your mind's eye.

* Replace my purpose with your own.

Tarot Association: The Sun's Face

The tarot card Major Arcana XIX, the Sun, corresponds with the lion's tail. This card represents the sun found within us; the spiritual sun that shines light on our sixth sense, or intuition. This is important because the five senses that we know so well—sight, hearing, smell, touch, and taste—are found collectively within the intuition. The Sun awakens the Self's inner senses, which, in turn, help us to manipulate our thoughts with greater skill, utilizing them to become adept at goal creation and to ultimately find new possibilities.

The Hebrew letter *Resh* is associated with the Sun card. Interestingly, *Resh* loosely translates into English as "face." All five senses can be found on the face: lips pertaining to touch, ears to hearing, nose to smelling, mouth to tasting, and eyes to seeing. The face also directs our consciousness, which, in turn, tells us that our goal directs our consciousness. The inner sun illuminates our path and gives us clear vision to see where we are going.

In magic, clear vision, or *clairvoyance*, is associated with the interior eyes, or mind's eye. Once open, the mind's eye becomes a gateway to the inner world where the process of putting together thoughts and goals takes place. Using the magic of the Sun card helps to develop this inner eye.

Although the Egyptian god Osiris was not associated with the sun directly, his famed regeneration by his wife and sister, Isis, and his intimate connection with vegetation and its cycle of regrowth makes him a powerful symbol of resurrection. It was believed that the sun resided in the underworld at night and came back again in the morning. This continuous resurrection symbolizes of the cycle of our thoughts being made manifest. Just as our desire is born in the mind's eye and reborn onto the Earth plane, another arises in place of it. So it is to Osiris and the sun that we turn to in order to be given understanding and control over the process of clear vision. The following meditation is the first step in awakening this inner sense by helping you make a conscious decision to use it.

VISUALIZATION EXERCISE

THE SUN: (FACE THE PRESENT)

Use this guided meditation as an initiation into your interior self. It can be done quickly in the morning or at night before you go to sleep.

In this meditation, you will be visualizing a house. It can be your own or imaginary. The house symbolizes your psyche, and each room represents a different state of awareness. For example, the basement represents an area where fears accumulate. It has very little, if any natural light and may be a place you go to escape from problems as well. It also represents the past. In a positive aspect, it represents your foundation and what lies at the root of a problem.

To begin, put a handful of eyebright (an herb associated with the sun) into a bowl and place it on your altar as an offering to Osiris. Go in to a relaxed state, and say,

Osiris, lord of Truth, touch me, awaken that which is asleep within and guide me towards the light.

Imagine that you are in the basement of your house waking from a nap. Slowly get up from the sofa where you

were slumbering and walk up the stairs to the main floor. Once there, you notice that you still have your eyes closed and are standing in darkness. You notice a faint glimmer of light through your eyelids and turn directly toward it. You have pivoted 180 degrees. Suddenly, you hear yourself say,

Now I choose to see!

At these words, you open your eyes and realize that you are facing east watching the rising sun. Its rays are pouring in through a large picture window, blessing you with warmth and purity. The house is flooded with light. You have a clear vision of your surroundings. You are facing the present.

Open your eyes. Thank Osiris for his help and throw the eyebright to Mother Earth. Log any experiences in your magic journal.

Enhancements for the Advanced Student

 * Bless a yellow candle with pure virgin olive oil. Carve the Hebrew letter *Resh* into it using a citrine point. Light it as an offering to Osiris before beginning the meditation (you may either extinguish the candle with a candle snuffer or let it burn out naturally).

 * Perform on a Sunday, on a full moon, or when the moon is in the sign of Leo. Perform on a solar eclipse.

 * Learn more about the Sephirah Tiphareth on the Qabalistic Tree of Life.

Alchemical Explanation:
The Alchemy of Creation

The lion's tail corresponds to alchemical sulfur. In alchemy, sulfur represents our spirit or inner essence. This is the energy of desire. It is that energy that makes us want to keep living. It can take on a primal nature, one of survival, but without it there would be no life. This energy represents the alchemical experience of giving birth to a goal and realizing what we desire, thus creating a starting point. Without this starting point, no magic could be put into action.

Another way to understand alchemical sulfur is to think of it as your personality. If you were to compare your personality to an essential oil, what would it be? Spicy and sweet like clove, wild and seductive like musk, or maybe welcoming and refreshing like lime? Trying to discern your personality helps teach you who you are. As you search, strong points will accentuate themselves, which you will be able to use in magic and other avenues of your life to achieve success.

Alchemical sulfur is composed of fire and air—two elements that can take you airborne. Imagine a hot air balloon for a moment. The fire heats the air and the balloon begins to rise. This can be an alchemical metaphor for your career taking off. On a deeper level, it can be seen as your very essence lifting your spiritual vehicle to great heights. If a hot air balloon is too slow or uncomfortable for you, replace it with an airplane. The same principle applies: air and fire, thought and desire.

On a higher level, this energy becomes more spiritual. The desire becomes strength, a potent energy force that Dragonflame helps transmute more easily, allowing us to notice that everyday struggles are spiritual and magical opportunities.

The more we work on ourselves spiritually, the closer we get to our pure essence or true will. This is what is meant by turning lead into gold: taking advantage of every opportunity that comes your way to transmute yourself into a more enlightened being leads to the Philosopher's Stone.

visualization exercise
alchemy of creation: (born of fire)

On page 65, you learned a meditation using widdershins or counterclockwise spirals for releasing energy built up during the length of a ritual or exercise. You will be using the same concept in this meditation, only with the direction of the spirals reversed. The clockwise motion represents activating energy, the "building up" or "starting your goal into motion" portion. Bringing the spiral from a broad radius out of the universe and down to a point on the earth plane represents collecting universal life force and drawing it down to the physical where you give birth to your goal. You will be vibrating or calling out the archangelic name Uriel. Uriel (pronounced Or'-ree–el) is the angel who resides over the Qabalah (see more about this on page 135) and Mother Earth. The angel's name means Fire of God, alluding to dominance over the realm of spirituality. Calling Uriel's name activates change at the highest level of spirituality and is extremely powerful. Please call this angel's name with the utmost respect, because when you do, you are calling on the Fire of God to be poured through your body in order to burn away all dross, or that which is no longer needed.

Enter a relaxed state and begin the following guided meditation.

Imagine that you are floating in the middle of outer space. Notice all of the stars around you, flashing here and there. A desire to create, to find, and to fulfill your destiny stirs inside and you feel a forward movement. There is another urge within you—a desire to know, to understand. This desire is so overwhelming it surpasses time. It is so powerful it springs forth from your spirit a mighty archangelic name. You call forth in a long, drawn out cry, Oooooooorrrrrrr - reeeeeeeee - eeeeeelllllllll (Uriel), and begin to move more quickly as you start to make your first clockwise spiral downward towards Mother Earth. You cry out again to the ends of the universe, Oooooooorrrrrrr - reeeeeeeee - eeeeelllllllll (Uriel), and create a second spiral breaking into the Earth's atmosphere as you corkscrew downward, faster. Finally, with your last breath, you cry Uriel's name and at the same time make the third and last spiral, touching ground on to the soil made fertile by Isis. Your goal has been planted. You are the seed.

Open your eyes. Log any experiences or feelings in your magic journal.

Enhancements for the Advanced Student

✳ Light a brown candle to the archangel Uriel and place an offering of mandrake root on your altar to her (you may either extinguish the candle with a candle snuffer or let it burn out naturally). Throw the mandrake root outside, back to Mother Earth when you are finished. Never bury wax in the earth, as some books on Wicca would advise. It is bad for the environment. Instead, throw the wax in the garbage when it has cooled down completely.

✳ Research the archangel Uriel further.

Summary

This chapter brought the final piece of the triad of the Dragonflame philosophy into focus. The lion's tail is associated with goal-making on Dragonflame's anatomy. One of its most important lessons is that by creating a goal, we agree to meet our destiny halfway. Somehow, the act of pursuing our dream creates an energetically charged reaction from the universe. This, in turn, allows the universe to change the course of our goal for our betterment (as well as that of anyone else touched by the ripples of our goal), thus maintaining balance. This is best explained through the analogy of Christopher Columbus's goal of finding a faster trade route to the East Indies. He set sail heading west to pursue his dream and instead accomplished another: landing in the Americas. This is further understood through the magical associations attributed to the lion's tail.

✳ **Astrological sign Leo (July 23–August 22).** The fiery astrological sign of Leo is best suited for the lion's tail because goals are fueled by our will. Strength, confidence, and creativity are three key ingredients in goal-making, which play out in the following manner: *strength* helps us follow through with a thought, *confidence* makes the decision-making process easier, and *creativity* expands our intellect by adding color, or "yin," energy to its otherwise masculine, or "yang," influence.

❊ **Tarot card Major Arcana XIX, the Sun.** On a subconscious level, the desire to create stirs our conscious mind into action. By studying Major Arcana XIX and utilizing the Dragonflame philosophy, we can awaken the sixth sense and pull original thought and life-changing goals directly from our inner sun.

❊ **The Hebrew letter Resh.** The spiritual sun found on the tarot card Major Arcana XIX awakens the inner senses to help manipulate thoughts with greater skill. Best understood in conjunction with the Hebrew letter *Resh*, translating into English as "face," this inner sun illuminates the face of our intuition and sixth sense.

❊ **The Egyptian god Osiris.** Although any slain and risen god or goddess may be associated with the lion's tail as found on Dragonflame, I have chosen Osiris, the Egyptian god of the dead and resurrection. The famous myth of Osiris illustrates a magical resurrection and a complete cycle, and is echoed in the Dragonflame philosophy. Osiris's body was torn into 14 pieces and scattered to the ends of the earth by his evil brother Set (also known as Apophis in the Greek pantheon). His wife and sister, Isis, found all the body parts with the exception of the phallus, and, through a series of magical events, aided Osiris's resurrection, making him the god of the underworld and rebirth. Quite simply, the myth parallels the thought or creation process:

   ❊ Isis symbolically gives birth to the thought process and creates purpose (by collecting Osiris's body and aiding in the resurrection process).

* Set or Apophis represents the sacrifice(s) necessary to bring the thought process into maturity, living the extent of its life and finally dying away (the tearing apart or death of Osiris).

* Osiris represents the new and/or refined thought that takes its place (the resurrection of Osiris, less the phallus, representing a more refined state of being).

* **Alchemical sulfur.** Alchemical sulfur represents our pure inner essence, defined as the personality. It creates desire and thus is a stimulus for goal-making. Its association with the lion's tail helps us understand the primal force within us that desires and wants, enabling our will to extend forth, reaching toward our goals. It is a necessary component in magic and naturally embedded in Dragonflame's philosophy and power.

Sometimes what we want is not necessarily what is best for us. Understanding the lion's tail and goal-making process will give you the tools and knowledge necessary to stop impeding change and allow you to mold your future as beneficially as possible. Consistent use of Dragonflame's Magical GPS System (Goal, Purpose, Sacrifice) will help you analyze your goals on a deeper level, bringing to light a more profound understanding of your desires, and whether they are best suited to your present needs.

A Summary of Dragonflame

1. **Lion's Tail**—The goal is your desire, wish, or dream.

2. **Unicorn's Horn**—The purpose is why you want that goal or what you will do with it once you obtain it. It is where the goal is found.

3. **Horse's Body**—The sacrifice is what you are willing to
    let go of in order to obtain your goal.

These three principles are the embodiment of the Dragonflame philosophy. The more you use them (with harm to none),
the more you will transform spiritually and refine your subtle
body (the Great Work), which eventually leads to the Philosopher's Stone (enlightenment).

Flame with Pentagram

Chapter 4

DRAGONFLAME INITIATION

Philosophical Explanation

Pluto's energy, the final component to the Dragonflame formula, lies at its plexus, kept hidden from those who might harm themselves inadvertently with its power. When you start using Dragonflame, Pluto's fiery energy is activated on a subconscious level and slowly rises to the surface of your consciousness in a safe manner. It pulls out what is not needed and burns away the dross, allowing your consciousness to put back together or re-assimilate the refined essence. Once this happens, you begin experiencing magic as a spiritual path and your goals start to manifest naturally, in accordance with Nature. This is also known as finding your True Will or knowing your purpose for this particular incarnation.

The only conscious effort necessary to use Pluto's energy is understanding and working with Dragonflame while keeping a pure purpose. Each time you define a purpose, goal, and sacrifice, Pluto will begin to hold up its end of the bargain—deep spiritual transformation and evolution. Pluto uncovers our vulnerability so Dragonflame may use it in the most beneficial manner.

Every time you use the Dragonflame philosophy, you refine your subtle body and strengthen your will by going through the process of separating the dross from the subtle and putting it back together again. Every time you follow this magical philosophy, you are doing what is known as the Great Work. In other words, every time you work magic using Dragonflame, you get closer to finding the Stone.

In magic, the element of fire is used to express magical development, transformation, and power. This is emphasized in Dragonflame's personality through the astrological force of Pluto. Fire, by its very nature, consumes and transforms. It is the only element that consistently needs another element to feed it: air. This much-needed air element is achieved through the momentum and movement created from sacrifice found in the Dragonflame formula. When mixed with a goal and purpose, a transformation is set in motion deep within the core of our own inner universe. This holy fire of transformation is the flame of the dragon, the same spiritual flame that changes philosophical lead into gold. Here's how it happens:

When all Dragonflame's working parts come together (goal, purpose, sacrifice), they create a transforming fire (Pluto) within our heart chakra where our True Will resides. The True Will is like a coal: once ignited, it burns on its own. It is the flame of love for the Divine, ignited from within. The flame from its embers is the Dragonflame.

mAGicAl exercise
ignitinG your true will

All processes, concepts, and energies found in the universe are also found within our own inner universe. These energies are expressed in magic through symbols and geometric shapes, which, in turn, are used to awaken the same latent energies within us. I designed this exercise to ignite your Dragonflame and to place you on your own path of creation. The following are some symbols and gods, along with their associations, which you will encounter along the way.

* **Upright Blue Pentagram:** This five-pointed star with one point directed upward is also known as a banishing pentagram. It is drawn in one line without lifting the pen from the paper (this is called a unicursal line). The star is drawn by starting at the lower left point and then by going consecutively to the upper most or top point, lower right (even with the lower left), upper left, upper right (even with upper left), and finally back to the lower left. Each point represents an element—earth, air, water, fire. The upward point represents the element of Spirit. When drawn with one point upward, it is a holy symbol meaning mind over matter. It signifies balance,

protection, and dominion over all the spirits, even the angels. When visualized in blue, it takes on the qualities of the planet Jupiter— expansion, philosophy, and mercy being just a few.

* **Upright Yellow-Gold Triangle:** This symbol represents the element of fire, transformation, and all trinities. When visualized in yellow-gold, it takes on solar qualities associated with the sun: Higher Self, higher astral, spirituality, life. The sun is also associated with the precious metal gold, representing the highest spiritual endeavors, and that which is incorruptible.

* **Zeus:** One of the ancient Greek gods (also known as Jupiter in ancient Rome), Zeus is called the God of the Gods. His archetype or universal energy represents wisdom, mercy, authority, guidance, wealth, and expansion.

* **Jesus:** Also known as Jesus Christ, he is one of the resurrected Gods and Ascended Masters. His archetype represents pure love, forgiveness, health, rebirth, Higher Self, salvation, refined essence, life everlasting, and balance. Jesus was crucified, buried, and rose from the dead, and is therefore part of the resurrection mythos, equivalent to the Egyptian god Osiris.

✴ **Spiral:** A spiral, or helix, represents the Goddess and expansion on all levels—spiritual, emotional, mental, and physical.

Nature creates in spirals. Even scientists agree about this phenomenon, caused by a magical number, *pi*, or the golden ratio. Hold on to this thought as you enter a relaxed state and follow the creative pattern of the universe in this next guided meditation.

Imagine you are standing facing east. In front of you is a flaming blue pentagram just shy of your height. Between you and it is your altar. Hear the sound the flame makes on the pentagram. Hear its voice. Feel its power. Slowly bring yourself into a lotus position, hovering in midair. You are a point in the universe. Turn 45 degrees so that you are facing south and begin to move forward following the line of a clockwise arc. As you turn the bend on this first spiral, you pick up speed. Feel the air rushing past you. Hear its voice. Now imagine a large triangle around your body in flaming yellow-gold. This triangle begins to crumble as you pick up momentum, and a new triangle takes its place within your heart chakra between your breasts—a smaller one, also in flaming yellow-gold. Become aware of a piece of coal within the center of this triangle. As you move faster, the rushing air ignites it. It is burning strongly as you approach the mid-point of your arc before the next homeward bend. Mentally say,

Zeus, show me what to do, and I'll do it so that I may accomplish the Great Work. So be it!

Thank you in advance.

Now you take the bend and arrive back in front of your altar, landing a little farther forward than where you first began. After all, you have expanded from having made one full spiral. As you stand in front of the flaming blue pentagram you see a vision of the face of Zeus in its upper triangle and Jesus in its center. Jesus is seated at the table where the Last Supper took place. He holds a chalice to you as if to say, "Drink." You understand his gesture as an invitation to enter into the mysteries, a decision that you must weigh. For once you drink from the grail, you have accepted your quest and cannot go back. Know that this is a holy quest whereby you agree to harm none and uphold the threefold law of the universe: what you send out will come back to you times three. Think about this for a while and make your decision to drink or not.

Open your eyes. Log any experiences in your magic journal.

Enhancements for the Advanced Student

✳ Study the path of Teth on the Qabalistic Tree of Life.

✳ Research the Sephiroth Chesed and Tiphareth on the Qabalistic Tree of Life.

✳ Assume the god form of Zeus throughout the guided meditation.

✳ Perform on a new moon.

✳ Perform when the moon is in Sagittarius and/or on a Thursday.

Creating the Dragonflame Talisman

I will provide two options for making the Dragonflame talisman: one round and using only geometric shapes and sigils, and the other rectangular and using geometric shapes, sigils, and Dragonflame's image. Both versions are drawn on parchment paper and are equally effective. Ultimately, it becomes a personal aesthetic choice. I prefer version two, however, because it resembles a tarot card. Perhaps one day Dragonflame will be Major Arcana XXII.

Version 1: Paper Talisman

Supplies: one sheet of virgin parchment paper, a pen, scissors, one bright yellow marker, and one sky blue marker.

Follow these steps:

1. Using the pen, begin by drawing a circle approximately 2 inches in diameter on the virgin parchment paper.

2. Draw a triangle, point upward, inside the circle, with each point touching its diameter.

3. In the center of the triangle, draw an elongated Hebrew letter Yod (ʼ) the height of the triangle.

4. In the three demilunes (the three half-moon shapes to the left, right, and below the triangle), draw the following three astrological glyphs: Virgo to the left, Scorpio to the right, and Leo at the bottom.

5. Using the scissors, cut around the perimeter of the circle to separate it from the page of parchment paper.

6. Turn the circle over (make sure the point on the triangle is upward before you turn it over) and draw the Hebrew letter Yod (ׁ) in the upper left and lower right corners, the Hebrew letter Nun (נ) in the upper right, across and center from the upper Yod, and the Hebrew letter Resh (ר) in the lower left, across and center from the lower Yod.

7. Turn it back over to the side with the triangle.

8. Using your markers, color the demilunes yellow and the triangle blue.

9. Laminate the talisman.

10. Hole-punch the top, triangle upward, if you would like to wear it around your neck during rituals, spells, and/ or meditations.

11. Consecrate your talisman (see page 108).

Version 2: Paper Talisman

Supplies: one sheet of virgin parchment paper, a pen, scissors, one bright yellow marker, one light gray marker, and one sky blue marker.

Follow these steps:

1. Using the pen, begin by drawing a rectangle approximately 3 inches wide by 4 inches high on the virgin parchment paper.

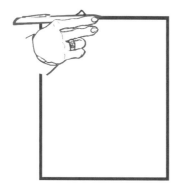

2. Using the scissors, cut around the perimeter of the rectangle to separate it from the parchment paper.

3. Draw three concentric circles centered onto the rectangle, each approximately 1/4 inch apart.

4. Color the outmost circle bright yellow, the next inward circle sky blue, and the innermost circle light gray.

5. Using the pen, draw the image of Dragonflame (a unicorn, rampant, with a tail in the shape of the astrological glyph of Leo) onto the rectangle, trying to center it as closely as possible in the central, light gray target.

6. Turn the paper over (make sure Dragonflame's head is upright before you turn it over) and draw the Hebrew letter Yod (ʼ) in the upper left and lower right corners, the Hebrew letter Nun (נ) in the upper right, across and center from the upper Yod, and the Hebrew letter Resh (ר) in the lower left, across and center from the lower Yod.

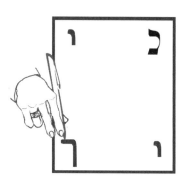

7. In the middle of the rectangle, in the shape of a triangle, draw the astrological glyphs as follows: Virgo as the top point of the triangle, Leo as the left point, and Scorpio as the right point.

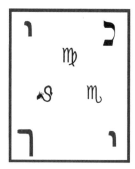

8. Laminate the talisman.

9. Hole-punch the top, triangle upward, if you would like to wear it around your neck during rituals, spells, and/ or meditations.

10. Consecrate your talisman (see page 108).

At this point in the book, you should have a good understanding of how the astrological glyphs and Hebrew letters fit into the Dragonflame philosophy. Their presence on your talisman will begin to hold deeper meaning as you use the Magical GPS system as presented in this book, and, in time, will create a personal bond among all of your bodies (physical, emotional, mental, spiritual) and Dragonflame's as well.

The colors used in the talisman also hold special meanings. They are Dragonflame's aura. As all the parts of Dragonflame begin to interact with one another, they create a trio of colors— light gray, sky blue, and bright sun yellow. Here are some of their associations:

* **Blue—The Color of Spirituality.** Sky blue, the color of clarity, spirituality, and serenity, belongs especially to the concept of Purpose. The color blue is associated with the Sephirah Chesed and represents good fortune, health, and expansion of philosophy.

* **Gray—The Color of Desire.** Craving a goal on a deep level can create a frenzy of desire, triggering us to utilize our entire being or essence in order to achieve our desired end. This means that we use our shadow self along with all other aspects of who we are—good and bad—when we work magic or deeply desire something. The color gray represents the mixed state of our being, our white and black sides flowing together, and belongs especially to the concept of Sacrifice. Fortunately, the Dragonflame philosophy teaches us to analyze our motivations and better understand our shadow self, allowing us to integrate their power into our magic safely and with awareness. The color gray is also associated with the Sephirah Chokmah and represents knowledge and wisdom.

* **Yellow—The Color of the Sun.** Achieving our desired result in a balanced fashion creates a chemical reaction releasing self-esteem, happiness, and confidence. A beautiful, golden yellow emanates from Dragonflame's aura like the sun, always shining light on the correct direction. Bright golden-yellow represents our Higher Self and belongs especially to the concept of Goals. The color yellow is associated with the Sephirah Tiphareth and represents creativity, beauty (within and without), recognition, balance, and health.

Consecrating the Dragonflame Talisman

May your love be pure
May your will be strong
Where the two become three
So mote it be.

—L. Leo

Goal: Manifest your highest aspirations.

Purpose: So that you may better serve Creator.

Sacrifice: Commitment to bettering yourself.

Supplies: Dragonflame talisman, Dragon's Blood oil or Dragon's Blood resin, mortar and pestle, plate (large enough to hold your talisman), about half a cup of salt, and four white votive candles (one for each quadrant of the compass—north, south, west, east).

Duration: One day (The number 1 is associated with the highest and most pure energy in the Practical Qabalah as well as Mother Earth. It symbolizes spirit and the beginning, and implies *another.*)

Offering: Burn nine drops of Dragon's Blood oil in your diffuser as an offering to Dragonflame. You can substitute the oil with Dragon's Blood resin (dragon's blood is associated with Pluto and transformation, the core of the Dragonflame philosophy).

It is not necessary to have a Dragonflame talisman to perform the spells or rituals in this book, but making a Dragonflame talisman does make a difference. From the moment of its consecration, it becomes a living entity on the astral realm.

The more you use it, the more powerful it will become. And, in return, the more potent and accurate your magic will become. With that said, if you made one, please take the time to consecrate it before you delve any deeper into the rituals contained in this book. Our lives are a reflection of our thoughts. We create our own universe. As we begin to release our goals into the astral, they take orbit about us and become integral parts of our personality and affect others who come into close enough proximity. This is why it is so important to create constructively through magic. What you put out there will come back to you.

Consecrating the Dragonflame talisman, whichever version you chose, will serve a twofold purpose: One, it will protect your karma through its alignment with the highest purpose possible, the Great Work. And two, it will allow you to use it for whatever goal you like, whenever you like. Most talismans serve only one goal. The Dragonflame talisman can be used for any goal or purpose.

Phases of the Moon

All the magical qualities of the moon (as well as the Earth, the Universe, and the Qabalah) are captured within the Dragonflame talisman. Through consecration, you place these energies under your will and awaken Dragonflame's essence or spirit. It becomes alive and acts as your familiar, or what I prefer to call your Spirit Companion. The moon is also associated with the cycle of life as we know it—birth, death, and rebirth. This same cycle is reflected through the archetype of the Triple Goddess—maiden, mother, and crone.

In Her new, or "maiden," phase, the moon represents goddesses such as Artemis and Diana (Greek and Roman pantheons), inspiring truth, knowledge, and justice in all who ask with a pure heart. This phase rules new beginnings, projects, and initiation of ideas.

In Her full, or "mother," phase, the moon represents goddesses such as Mary (Christian) and Isis (Egyptian pantheon), bestowing health, love, marriage, wealth, general wishes, and all good things.

In Her dark, or "crone," phase, the moon represents goddesses such as Circe and Hecate (Greek pantheon) and abstract energies such as wisdom, endings, death, silence, and all things of a hidden or even dark nature. This should not frighten you. These energies exist in our earthly reality. Remain ignorant of their powers and they will rule you; study their powers and you will have a better chance at ruling them. A healthy respect grants illumination and control.

During all of Her phases, the moon (considered a planet by the ancients and in the Practical Qabalah) is the closest celestial body to us, and at times, one of the most visible as well. Her proximity makes Her the most logical choice from which to change your philosophical and psychic perspective and to jump-start psychic development. Here's a quick creative visualization to help:

Imagine you are the moon for a moment. You are shining brightly at your zenith up in the night sky. Fix your gaze upon planet Earth. Everyone sees you, or at least knows you are there, for every face, of every race, in every nation sees the moon. A powerful energy emanates from you toward the Earth and every person walking its surface. You watch over them, but yet are not of them, separate from the Earth's time and worries. There is no concern of money, work, or fulfilling desires of any sort. You simply orbit about, hearing and seeing all that the human race does and thinks. You observe. You illuminate their minds and store all their subconscious thoughts and desires. Your landscape may appear to be dead, but it is powerfully alive with psychic energy, working with shadow and light, ever waxing and waning.

Altar Arrangements and Instructions

✳ Mix nine drops of Dragon's Blood oil and a pinch of Dragon's Blood resin in your mortar with half a cup of salt. Using the pestle, grind the mixture for approximately five minutes while chanting,

Teach me how to channel all of the positive energies of Dragonflame so that I may use them to my advantage.

✳ Place either your oil diffuser or incense (dragon's blood resin) on the upper left corner. If you are using an oil diffuser, put nine drops of Dragon's Blood oil in it.

✳ Place the Dragonflame talisman on a plate and center it on the altar.

✳ Make a circle around the perimeter of the plate with the Dragon's Blood/salt mixture.

	White Candle (East)	
White Candle (North)	Dragonflame Talisman on Plate	White Candle (South)
	White Candle (West)	
Oil Diffuser		

✳ Light the votives in a clockwise manner, starting with the candle in the south and ending with the candle in the east. Say this Consecration Affirmation:

> *With all the power in me and with all my heart and soul, I, [state your name or magical name], hereby consecrate this talisman to manifesting my highest aspirations and goals. With harm to none and for the greatest good of all so that I may better serve Creator.*

After the consecration, place your Dragonflame talisman in a safe place wrapped in white cloth (100-percent silk or cotton is best). Wear it around your neck or place it on the altar during all your magical workings to increase power and success. Remember, the more you use the Dragonflame talisman, the more powerful it will become. To help bond with it, you may want to meditate on its magical attributes.

Building a Rapport with Dragonflame

Hold the talisman in your hand and concentrate on its aspects one by one. What does deep spiritual transformation mean to you? Describe a metaphorical cycle of birth, death, and renewal that has taken place in your life. Think of the full moon's associations of power and psychic impressions. What kind of psychic impressions do you want to imprint your talisman with? Ask your questions one by one and sit in silence listening for the answers. It may come to you in a vision, voice, or even a feeling of knowing. Be patient with yourself and try the meditation as often as you like. To help better understand Dragonflame, create a question-and-answer entry in your magic journal using the following questions. After using Dragonflame for several months, revisit this entry and see if any of the answers have changed or remained the same.

* Do I associate the color sky blue with any emotions? If so, which ones?

* Do I associate the color gray with any emotions? If so, which ones?

* Do I associate the color yellow with any emotions? If so, which ones?

* What transformation(s) has taken place in my life so far?

* Have I ever analyzed my motivations behind wanting a particular goal?

Choose a mid- or long-term goal (perhaps one from the rituals in Chapter 6 beginning on page 143), and ask yourself what the repercussions would be for everyone involved if you obtained it. Follow the chain of events as far as you can.

Another way to build a rapport with your talisman is to light a candle or offering to it. You can light a candle to Dragonflame on any day or night, but the night of the dark, new, or full moon is most powerful.

On the new moon, light a black-and-white candle to signify the end of an old cycle and the beginning of a new one. Also, purchase fresh basil and place a few sprigs in a small glass of water. Place it on your altar or your kitchen table as an offering to Dragonflame. Basil can be used to create or strengthen a bond with dragons, banish fear, and bring courage and protection.

On the dark moon leading into the new moon and the night of the new moon, light a black candle to Dragonflame and imagine yourself as a snake shedding its skin. Ask Dragonflame to cover you with a shroud as dark as midnight and protect you from all harm, psychic or otherwise.

On the full moon, light a red candle signifying power, strength, and commitment. Red is such a powerful color. It is the color of our blood, the vital common denominator of all humans. It symbolizes sustenance, life, and mystery. Think of those associations while you use Dragon's Blood oil to bless the candles.

You can also light some Dragon's Blood resin/incense or burn some oil in a diffuser as an offering to Dragonflame. You can do this whenever you like and as often as you like. This is your way of feeding your thought form. Through these acts, you will keep Dragonflame alive and thriving on the astral realm, and it will more willingly bestow its positive influences upon you on the physical realm.

The act of consecrating your talisman has now set you upon a deeply powerful and transformational path—one of integrity and truth that will guide you to your true purpose and help you find yourself along the way. If I may borrow, and loosely manipulate, a verse out of Jules Verne's *Journey to the Center of The Earth*: Descend, bold traveler, into the depths of your being, and you will attain the center of the Earth.

Enhancements for the Advanced Student

- Perform on a Tuesday (the day of Mars).
- Perform during the planetary hour of Mars.
- Perform during the full moon.

✸ You can also use the Dragonflame talisman to power-fully enhance the LBRP (Lesser Banishing Ritual of the Pentagram), and BRH (Banishing Ritual of the Hexagram). (See the Glossary and Recommended Reading sections.) Simply wear it around your neck or place it on your altar.

Summary

This chapter brought all three elements of Dragonflame together (Goal, Purpose, Sacrifice) to reveal a fourth element lying at its heart—Pluto, or deep spiritual transformation. The goal of this chapter has been to deepen your relationship with Dragonflame. This is done through the Dragonflame initiation, learning how to make the Dragonflame talisman, and the Dragonflame talisman consecration. Dragonflame teaches us how to properly combine specific aspects of our human nature in order to manifest our desires and become more spiritually refined through the process. As you embrace Dragonflame you also embrace the essence of magic and the nuts and bolts behind the power of creation. Dragonflame has very specific magical associations, most of which can only be understood through combination. Here is a brief reference:

✸ **Pluto.** Pluto is known as the planet of transformation. It is the ruling planet of Scorpio, so there is deep spirituality to be found through this particular energy. Its power is the driving force of and byproduct found at the center of Dragonflame.

✸ **The three phases of the moon.** The three phases of the moon (new, dark, full) represent the mystery of life—birth, death, and rebirth. Dragonflame utilizes and parallels this ideal through its magical philosophy:

* Birth of a Goal as it surfaces from the subconscious mind

* Death through Sacrifice of something lesser in order to achieve something greater (the goal)

* Rebirth of a refined Purpose and spirituality through experience and personal examination

* **The Hebrew letters Yod, Nun, and Resh, and the zodiac signs Virgo, Scorpio, and Leo.** Within the Dragonflame philosophy the three Hebrew letters Yod, Nun, and Resh embrace the same energy as Virgo, Scorpio, and Leo. Each Hebrew letter and astrological glyph represents an aspect of Dragonflame:

  * Goal—Resh, Leo

  * Purpose—Yod, Virgo

  * Sacrifice—Nun, Scorpio

* A continuous cycle of birth-death-rebirth and goal-purpose-sacrifice occurs by duplicating the first letter/glyph of each trio and adding it in succession. For example: Yod, Nun, Resh, Yod (ירני) and Virgo, Scorpio, Leo, Virgo (♍ ♏ ♌ ♍). In this way, continuous movement, change, and evolution are signified, explaining the deep transformation and Pluto's invisible existence within the Dragonflame philosophy.

* **The colors gray, sky blue, and bright yellow.** Three colors are associated with Dragonflame to identify its aura: light gray, sky blue, and bright yellow. Light gray is a mixture of black and white, reminding us that our desires are never as simple as good and bad. Dragonflame teaches to examine motives and understand the shadow and light selves, so that we may wield magic

properly. Sky blue signifies health, spirituality, purpose, and peace. Bright yellow represents the light of the sun, our Higher Self, and the Philosopher's Stone.

Embarking on the path of magic quickens evolution. Make Dragonflame your spiritual companion to help guide you. Ask Dragonflame to help you find the most beneficial course to creativity, freedom, and spirituality. Return to this chapter whenever you feel the need to reestablish and/or help maintain a healthy rapport with Dragonflame.

Vitruvian Man

CHAPTER 5

THE MECHANICS OF YOUR INTERIOR SPACES

The Magic Circle

In its simplest form, a magic circle is a circle that you draw around yourself before performing a ritual. The circle can be imaginary (white light, fire), physical (string, salt, water), or both. Traditionally, it is used to cleanse your working space of unwanted energies, to define a boundary line of protection, and to create a focal point or center from which to work. The magic circle also has a more complex, philosophical meaning.

Within it lies the entirety of your inner universe: all that you know and do not know, all that you have explored and have yet to explore; galaxies, planets, suns, the zodiac—everything that you can dream of or possibly conceive. Stars are born within your circle; supernovas occur within it. It is the sum total of the universe and all its parts, and *you* define its perimeter.

There are many purposes served by the magic circle, including, but not limited to: protection, providing a sacred space to do your magical workings, introspection, and magical progress. But by far the most important purpose of the magic circle is separation.

When you cast a magic circle, you define a particular space as separate from all other space outside of its circumference. The very act separates you from:

1. Everyday consciousness.

2. The mundane world.

3. That aspect of the self as defined by society, also known as the ego (For example, you may be called a brother, sister, father, mother, husband, wife, lover, plumber, judge, lawyer, or priest. These are all man-made terms, created by society. They do not exist within the magical circle. You, the magician, high priest, witch, priestess, and so on, exist within it, and, if you're lucky enough to know it, your magical name also exists within its perimeter.)

4. Outside influences and unwanted and/or negative energies, such as stress, worry, upset, and so on.

5. A microcosmic perspective. (In other words, it takes you from the perspective of being in a particular location on the planet Earth and into a perspective of being the center of your own universe looking at the planet Earth as well as all the other planets.)

As you begin to understand that the entire universe exists within the magic circle or sphere, then the question will arise, what lies beyond its borders? Creator. This simple word represents a concept and a force which we cannot conceive of or name. Creator made the sphere and everything inside it, including us (in the sense of a link to our Higher Self). Adopting this mindset and having the desire to transcend the universe results in your coming to know Creator by knowing yourself. And this, in essence, is magical progress.

With this knowledge, making the magic circle is very easy. It is simply an act of putting up and taking down, or separating and putting back together again. Creating a magic circle is the magician's way of saying, "I am lost no more. I have a goal and purpose. Here is my first point of focus." I call it invoking the Goddess Urania because in ancient Greece she was worshipped as the goddess of the heavens or universe.

Before casting your magic circle, be sure to choose a room that can be properly secured from any threats to your concentration and the successful completion of your circle. Close and lock the door and windows to prevent intrusion, and turn the phone off or put it on silent to prevent interruption. If you have any pets, make sure they are content and in another room. In magic, this is known as *tilling the chamber*.

The main reason for tilling the chamber is to prevent someone from breaking or crossing your magic circle. It is a bad omen if this should happen and can create a mild to severe imbalance on all levels—spiritual, emotional, mental, and physical. The circumference of the magic circle becomes a membrane, allowing the side-by-side existence of two different states of being. When you first begin practicing magic, this membrane is very fragile. Should it be ruptured, magical reality and physical reality (the subconscious and conscious mind) impinge upon one another freely. This can be compared to being asleep and awake at the same time, allowing subconscious images to float into the consciousness without control. The circumference of the magic circle also creates an intimate space where you hide your secrets, nurture your goals, and feel most secure. Having it crossed or broken will leave an uncomfortable sense of vulnerability and violation. For these reasons, it is important to properly cast your circle, then do your magical workings, and finally take it down properly before returning to routine, mundane duties.

As you continue practicing magic, your circle will become stronger due to repetition and the increase in the power of your will. This does not mean that you are exempt from the consequences if it is crossed or broken. It does mean, however, that it can act as a magical alarm system, warning of approaching harm or danger. For example, I have noticed, after years of practicing magic, that the magic circle has taken root in my subconscious mind and on the astral realm. One lucid dream stands out in particular: A close friend suddenly barged through a secure door and broke my circle. Angrily, I dismissed him, closed the door, and went back to the business at hand. I woke up remembering the experience with dread, wondering what it meant and waiting for some grave consequence. Several days later, I threw my lower back out. My friend (the same one from the lucid dream) came rushing over with a bottle of pain relievers to save the day. Against my better judgment and in unbearable pain I took one. I was sick from the medication for the entire evening. The next day, semi-recovered, I threw the bottle away. My lucid dream was prophetic: it foretold an error in judgment, but also left room for correction.

Creating the Magic Circle: Invoking the Goddess Urania

Standing facing east, with your altar in front of you, point your right forefinger at the center of the wall in front of you. Imagine a white light, like a white flame, flowing down through your head, neck, and arm, and out your forefinger. Slowly, pivot 360 degrees clockwise, drawing the circumference of your magic circle with the white flame. Mentally, extend the circle to the outermost points of the room while you are turning. Be sure to end at your starting point and connect the circle completely. You may relax your hand.

Now, turn your magic circle into a sphere and visualize it as a hologram of the universe with you at its center. This is the true reality. The external one we live in, also known as reality, is its reflection.

Do your magical working(s)/prayerwork.

When you have finished, reabsorb your magic circle. This time, you will use your left forefinger. Point it at the wall in front of you where your circle began. Slowly, pivot 360 degrees counterclockwise while imagining the white flame being absorbed back into your being via the left forefinger. When you are done, bring your hands together in what is called prayer position in front of your heart chakra located between your breasts. This is done by placing your palms together with your fingers pointed upward.

The Altar: As Above, So Below

Altars can be found all around the world, from Catholic churches to Buddhist temples, and even in the house next door. In fact, many altars are found in the kitchen because that room is usually considered the heart of the home. But no matter where your altar is located, the same rule applies: Your physical altar is a macrocosmic reflection of the one located at the center of your microcosmic universe.

That's right—you have an altar in your interior space as well as your exterior one. The altar is the outward manifestation of this inner point. It acts as a link or bridge between these two worlds. This means that whatever is found on your altar should hold a deeply symbolic meaning to you. Each item, image, color, or fragrance should hold enough meaning to trigger or stir your emotional state intensely. It must be powerful enough to awaken and attract energy from the universe, from the spiritual realm, and from within your heart. Your altar is a focal point not just for your thoughts and emotions, but for your spirit as well. By treating it as such, you begin the process of manifesting thought into matter.

What you place on your altar will sooner or later be attracted into your physical realm of being. This follows a simple rule: like attracts like. If it is love you want to attract, a simple but effective way to start would be to place a pink heart on your altar. Whatever you look at every day and focus on every day, you will attract into your life. Your altar is like a star that pulls your desires into its orbit like planets around our sun.

Procuring your altar is one of your first acts of magic. It follows an ancient axiom or law of the universe: "as above, so below." A very simple translation of this would be "what you think is what you manifest." When you create an altar, you are saying to the universe, "I have found that area within myself where I am most centered." And, in turn, the universe responds, "I have guided you here." By carving out a spiritual location in your environment, you have enabled your ideas or goals to become reality.

The altar and your goal are opposite poles and are therefore attracted to one another. The altar represents the first and the last stage of the magical process; the place where your goal begins to harden into reality. Imagine your goal as having worked its way down from the spiritual, emotional, and mental planes and finally to the physical via your altar. This happens because you have an area to direct it towards, an area where all your magical pieces come together in one place so your spirit and other spirits can touch it and bring it to life. Remember, your altar is an area of spiritual influx set aside from the mundane. It will attract spirits who vibrate at the same level of your purpose, whether high or low, good or bad.

Another important concept of the altar is balance. Traditionally, the altar is where you will place physical representations of the four elements of creation: air, fire, water, and earth. Each of these elements resides within you. If one of them is out of balance, it manifests outwardly in a negative fashion. Unfortunately, imbalance is a necessary evil. Without it, we could never understand the true meaning of balance. Fortunately, the Dragonflame philosophy reminds us that imbalance is temporary and can be remedied through purpose. This is reflected on your altar through purposeful action and placement. In other words, every object is placed on your altar with awareness and intention. Your altar then becomes a powerful and safe area for manifestation to occur.

Throughout this book, you are given a variety of altar arrangements for each ritual and spell. Use them as guidelines for your own spells and rituals. Experiment with your intuitions. Perhaps your eye is naturally attracted to a balanced format and you like having two candles rather than one. If so, go with that feeling. Play with different colors, textures, flowers, herbs, gems, pictures—anything that moves you. Remember, from this point on, everything you place on your altar has a meaning.

Many of those meanings are covered in magical books and grimoires, but the most important meaning is the one you assign.

Blessing or Dressing a Candle

Until you bless or dress a candle, it is just plain wax. Dressing infuses it with the active energies contained in your desire or wish. This is also known as *charging* a candle.

This technique of dressing a candle is a hybrid of the Dragonflame methodology and a version taught to me by a dear friend and mentor, Mary Glomb, who has since passed away. It teaches you how to instill both goal and purpose within the candle. I will use an example with the goal of attracting success and the purpose of peace of mind to illustrate the mechanics more easily:

Hold the candle with the wick up (facing the ceiling). Using your index finger, place the desired oil on the middle of the side of the candle facing you and stroke upwards, saying the goal,

With all the power in me and with all my heart and soul, I, [state your name or magical name] hereby bless this candle with the goal of attracting success.

Turn the candle with the wick down (facing the floor). Again, place your index finger in the middle of the candle and stroke upwards (toward the bottom of the candle) saying the purpose,

So that I may have peace of mind.

Turn the candle right side up once more, squeeze the wick between your forefinger and thumb, and say,

So be it!

Once your candle is dressed, you can place it on the altar to be lit during the spell or ritual.

For future use, simply replace the goal and purpose with your own and use the proper oil associated with them as well.

Extinguishing a Candle

Always extinguish a candle's flame by using a candlesnuffer. This shows respect for the element of fire, also known as *fire wise*.

Cleansing and Consecrating Objects

Consecrating an item means to imbue it with a special purpose. This is usually done in conjunction with an item whose magical association matches your purpose. For example, if you would like to attract love, a suitable gemstone to use would be rose quartz. If you would like to attract prosperity, perhaps you might use aventurine. Whatever the choice, any item that you would like to use as a magical tool must first be cleansed of negativity. This preparation makes it receptive to your magical energy.

Items often become targets for people's intentions and thoughts. Every time you hold, pick up, or even look at an object, you imbue it with your energy—either consciously or subconsciously, subtly or forcefully. For example, when a child walks into a store and sees an object that he or she wants badly, that child unconsciously marks it through the psychic stress created by his or her desire. Although an innocent act, the object is charged nonetheless. And, if needed for a spell or ritual, that item would have to be cleansed and made neutral so it could be charged with a new psychic impression without the old one getting in the way.

There are many ways to cleanse an object of negativity, positivity, or an energetic imprint. Using each of the four elements for this purpose is a powerful solution. Remember, "long and involved" does not make a cleansing better. It is all about your intent and knowledge. Here are some quick and efficient ways to cleanse an object using the four elements:

1. **Fire:** Pass the object through or over the flame of a candle or a small, contained fire.

2. **Air:** Pass the object through the smoke created by burning incense or through the steam from an oil diffuser. Or simply blow on the object or use a fan or feather.

3. **Earth:** Place your object in a bowl filled with salt for 30 to 60 minutes.

4. **Water:** Place the object under running water. You can do this by holding it under the faucet in the kitchen sink if you wish. A few seconds will be sufficient.

A few notes: Some minerals, such as citrine, do not require cleaning. Others, such as kyanite and malachite, should not be immersed in salt or in water. Do not heat a stone and then place it in cold water, as this could cause the stone to shatter.

Whatever element or technique you choose, it will be effective if you follow this GPS:

Goal: *Cleanse this object of all negativity* (or stale energy).

Purpose: *So it may be a proper receptacle for my will.*

Sacrifice: The sacrifice is going to be whichever element you use to cleanse your object and the time it takes you to complete the cleansing.

Begin the cleansing process by holding the object in your hand (right or left, whichever feels better to you) and say the following Cleansing Affirmation:

> *With all the power in me and with all my heart and soul I, [state your name or magical name], cleanse this object of all negativity and evil.*

Now pass it through the flame/smoke/water or sprinkle some salt on it each time you say the following:

Not once, not twice, but thrice. So be it!

Now that the object has been purified, it is ready to be charged or imbued with your intent.

Using a Consecration Circle

Obtain a plate large enough to hold your chosen object. Place six white votives around the plate, evenly spaced. Outside this, make a circle following the perimeter of the plate with salt. The salt keeps negativity outside the circle and your intent within the circle. This is also reinforced by the six white votives. Six is a number associated with the Higher Self, balance, and the Sun on the Qabalistic Tree of Life.

Light the votives and say this Consecration Affirmation:

> *With all the power in me and with all my heart and soul I, [state your name or magical name], hereby consecrate this [state the name of the object, such as crystal or candle] to [state the goal, such as to attract success]. With harm to none and for the greatest good of all so that I may [state your purpose, such as have peace of mind].*

Allow the candles to burn for an hour or so, or let them burn out naturally, and throw the salt back to Mother Earth. You are finished.

Thanking and Releasing the Spirits

At the end of any spell or ritual you must always thank the spirits and release them. This process allows you to psychologically let go as well. If you are just starting to work magic and cannot feel or see the presence of any spirits, it may be a bit difficult at first. Thanking and releasing what appears to be nothing may give you the tendency to rush or feel doubtful. Until you have your first experience with the spirits, the best antidote is to imagine that you are thanking a good friend for stopping by and helping you with something in the house.

Here is my "thanks and release," which is based on a spiritual hierarchy. I bow as far as I can when I thank Creator, midway when I thank the Gods and Goddesses, and nod my head to the spirits and elementals.

Begin by saying,

> *Thank you Creator, to whom I choose to return, serve, and worship only.*

Bow as far as you can and then return to standing position after a small pause.

Bow again mid-way and say,

> *Thank you Gods, Goddesses.* (Angels and saints fit into this category as well.)

Return to standing position.

Nod after each when you say:

> *Thank you Spirits, Elementals, all who have helped me here now.*

This completes the "thank you" portion. Next is the "release" portion. This particular release is adapted from Donald Michael Kraig's version in his wonderful book *Modern Magick: Eleven Lessons in the High Magickal Art* (p. 258):

> *I now release all spirits who have shared in this ceremony. May there always be peace between us. May you always walk alongside me. Or, if you wish, return now to your natural habitats and help someone else along the way. So be it.*

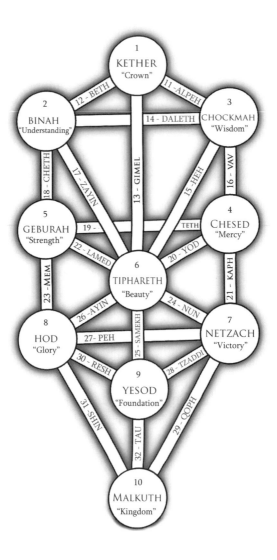

The Tree of Life with Paths.

Vibrating the God Names

The ancient Greek playwright Euripides was supposed to have written the adage "the tongue is mightier than the blade." If indeed he did, then he knew something great about the world of magic. Voice, sound, and vibrations are powerful tools when applied to the occult, as long as you know how to manipulate them properly.

As humans we have the ability to think, speak, or write words. In magic, when we speak them, either internally or outwardly, this is called *working with the Logos*. In the first book of the Old Testament, Genesis 1:3, God created with the Logos: "And God said, 'let there be light'; and there was light." In the New Testament, the Gospel of John also describes creation with the Logos: "In the beginning was the Word, and the Word was with God and the Word was God."

It is not as easy as that, of course. But with some knowledge, understanding, and practice, you can incorporate the vibration of Power Words or God Names into your spells, rituals, and meditations.

To begin, you must alter your thinking to understand that any God Name or Power Word (or energy, for that matter) already exists within your own microcosm. This new thought process allows you to choose whatever energy you like and awaken or activate it through intoning or vibrating it either out loud or mentally. For example, if success is what you are trying to attract, then you might choose the god name El, corresponding to the planet Jupiter and Sephirah Chesed from the Qabalistic Tree of Life. By vibrating it, either out loud or to yourself, you are awakening its corresponding energy already residing within you.

If you have no idea what a god name is or what power word to choose, not to worry. I have chosen the appropriate words for you and have placed them throughout the book, either in the body of the content or at the end of each exercise and/or ritual under Enhancements for the Advanced Student.

To make the vibration process more powerful, visualize the spelling of the god name or power word in your mind's eye. Then, inhale deeply through your nose and direct the air to stream down the back of your throat and into your lungs. Let your abdomen or stomach area expand first, as if the air is filling this area to capacity and then moving upward. Once you have taken in as much air as you can, hold the breath for two seconds. As you exhale, pronounce the god name or power word in a low tone with a vibrato or pulsating effect until there is no more air in your lungs. It should sound as if you are calling out to the ends of the universe as your chosen word crosses the barriers of time, making a change within your interior world. It will help if you imagine the name you are vibrating is a giant gong that you are beating slowly and rhythmically. The vibration coming from the gong is your god name, a current of energy. Whatever is next to it will also be set into motion through a law of physics called sympathetic vibrations.

Most magic utilizing the Qabalistic Tree of Life usually involves a series of words that need to be vibrated. It adds great power to any ritual, spell, or meditation, as well as to your psyche. The majority of god names or power words are holy names in Hebrew and must be spoken with great respect. They are not evil in any way, shape, or form. In fact, they are neutral and will conform to your goal and purpose. In other words, you will reap what you sow.

The Practical Qabalah

Kabbalah is a Hebraic tradition outlining the creation of the universe on both a microcosmic and macrocosmic level (visible and invisible). In English it means "to receive," referring to the way its sacred knowledge was received by each generation through word of mouth. The more contemporary version, also called the Practical or Hermetic Qabalah (usually spelled *Qabalah* as opposed to the rabbinical *Kabbalah*), evolved from the Judaic Kabbalah, which has served as the underlying structure for many mystery schools and the Western esoteric tradition. *Dragonflame* is based on the Practical Qabalah, rather than the rabbinical Kabbalah.

The Qabalah teaches that creation takes place in ten steps. Each step is a sacred emanation of light issuing forth from Creator, called a *Sephirah*, that has its own level of consciousness. The Sephiroth (plural for Sephirah) have been named and associated with a planet or facet of the universe. They are placed in a sacred glyph known as the Tree of Life.

The Tree of Life can be further separated into three pillars, four worlds, three triads, and 32 paths, as follows:

The Three Pillars

The Middle Pillar represents balance and contains Kether, Tiphareth, Yesod, and Malkuth in descending order.

The Pillar of Severity (to the Middle Pillar's right) represents the female force and conscious mind and contains Binah, Geburah, and Hod in descending order.

The Pillar of Mercy (to the Middle Pillar's left) represents the male force and unconscious mind and contains Chockmah, Chesed, and Netzach in descending order.

The Four Worlds

Each Sephirah exists on four arcs or "levels of being," to which particular forces or energies are assigned:

1. Atziluth—the Archetypal World of Spirit and fire. A god name is assigned to each Sephirah.

2. Briah—the Creative World of emotions and water. An Archangel is assigned to each Sephirah.

3. Yetzirah—the Formative World of thoughts and air. A Choir of Angels is assigned to each Sephirah.

4. Assiah—the Active World of the mundane and earth. A natural force or energy is assigned to each Sephirah.

The 32 Paths

The Sephiroth have been connected in a particular fashion creating 22 lines, or "paths." Counting each of the 10 Sephiroth as well, the *32 paths of wisdom* are formed, creating a map of our soul—the magical universe (macrocosmic) and our internal universe (microcosmic). When we travel these paths, we "make" magic and speed up our evolutionary process.

The Three Triads

✴ **The Supernal Triangle.** The first three Sephiroth (Kether, Chockmah, Binah) are incomprehensible to the human mind. Together, they create what is known as the Supernal Triangle, the beginning of creation and the highest part of our soul.

✴ **The Ethical Triangle.** The next set of three Sephiroth (Chesed, Geburah, Tiphareth) create the Ethical

Triangle. Chesed's expansion and orderliness unite with Geburah's "winding-down" aspect and discipline. They balance each other as harmony within Tiphareth. It is here that ethics and morals are first created.

✳ **The Astral Triangle.** The last set of three Sephiroth (Netzach, Hod, Yesod) create the Astral Triangle: the triangle of the personality. The emotions of Netzach collide with the intellect of Hod to create the astral substance in Yesod. Here the personality is defined. The final Sephirah, Malkuth, is left by itself because it is the sphere that receives all of the emanations from the other Sephiroth.

Each of the 10 Sephiroth holds a host of magical associations and meanings. The following is a brief list giving the name of the Sephirah in Hebrew and then English, the number of the Sephirah, its location on the Tree, a brief description of its energy, and its macro- and microcosmic association and color (in queen scale). This is by no means a detailed analysis of the Hermetic Qabalah and should only be used to become acquainted with the Tree of Life or for a quick reference. If the reader would like a more thorough or in depth analysis, please see the References and Recommended Reading section on page 243.

1. **Kether, or "Crown."** The first Sephirah is located at the top of the Middle Pillar. This is the highest and most pure energy, where the light of Creator finds its first point of focus. Its macrocosmic association is the Primum Mobile or outermost concentric sphere of the universe. It is also the beginning of light or the "seed" light of a star. Microcosmically, or on the human body, it is associated with the cranium and brain. Kether's color is white.

2. **Chockmah, or "Wisdom."** The second Sephirah is located at the top of the Pillar of Mercy. It is here that the energy first takes on a gender and defines itself as masculine, projective, and a yang force and is known as the Great Abba or Father. Macrocosmically, it is associated with the zodiac in its entirety. Microcosmically, it is associated with the left side of the face. Chockmah's color is gray.

3. **Binah, or "Understanding."** The third Sephirah is located at the top of the Pillar of Severity. In this Sephirah, the energy transitions to feminine, receptive, and yin force and is known as the Great Amma or Mother. It is the first Sephirah where form emerges. Macrocosmically, it is associated with the planet Saturn. Microcosmically, it is associated with the right side of the face. Binah's color is black.

4. **Chesed, or "Mercy."** The fourth Sephirah is located in the middle of the Pillar of Mercy, under Chockmah. As Binah's energy overflows, it creates Chesed, the first Sephirah that the human mind can comprehend. Its energies are beneficent, orderly, and merciful, and encompassed by the Greek god Zeus. This is the "building up" or expanding energy found within the universe. Macrocosmically, it is associated with the planet Jupiter. Microcosmically, it is associated with the left arm. Chesed's color is blue.

5. **Geburah, or "Strength."** The fifth Sephirah is located in the middle of the Pillar of Severity, just under Binah. Geburah's energies are the opposite of Chesed: severe, aggressive, and merciless. They are encompassed by Mars, the Roman God of War. This is the "breaking down" or dissipating energy found within the universe.

Macrocosmically it is associated with the planet Mars. Microcosmically it is associated with the right arm. Geburah's color is red.

6. **Tiphareth, or "Beauty."** The sixth Sephirah is located at the center of the Middle Pillar, below Kether. Tiphareth, holding true to its name, is pure beauty, harmony, balance, and health. It is known as the Sephirah of the sacrificed gods, and its energy is encompassed by Jesus and Buddha. It is associated with spirituality, the Higher Self, and the Philosopher's Stone. Macrocosmically, it is associated with the sun. Microcosmically, it is associated with the solar plexus and breast area. Tiphareth's color is yellow.

7. **Netzach, or "Victory."** The seventh Sephirah is located at the bottom of the Pillar of Mercy, below Chesed. Netzach is all emotion, the creative aspect of the personality, and the instincts. This sphere, or sacred emanation, is associated with love and the Goddess Aphrodite. Macrocosmically, it is associated with the planet Venus. Microcosmically, it is associated with the loins, left leg, and left hip. Netzach's color is green.

8. **Hod, or "Glory."** The eighth Sephirah is located at the bottom of the Pillar of Severity, below Geburah. If Netzach is all emotion, then Hod is its opposite: all intellect. It is the sphere of thinking and is associated with symbols, sigils, books, and the science behind magic. The Roman God Mercury encompasses Hod's energies. Macrocosmically, it is associated with the planet Mercury. Microcosmically, it is associated with the loins, right leg, and right hip. Hod's color is orange.

9. **Yesod, or "Foundation."** The ninth Sephirah is located underneath Tiphareth on the Middle Pillar. This

is the sphere of the astral realm. It is called the foundation because the blueprint for all that exists on the earth realm first exists in Yesod, thus the axiom "as above, so below." Macrocosmically, it is associated with the moon. Microcosmically, it is associated with the reproductive organs. Yesod's color is violet.

10. **Malkuth, or "Kingdom."** The tenth Sephirah is located underneath Yesod at the base of the Middle Pillar. It is the polar opposite of Kether. This is the reality that we exist in presently, the three-dimensional Earth realm. Here all five elements (earth, air, water, fire, spirit) come together within us and without. It is the sphere of spirit encased within the material—hardened light. When we send out our will magically, it travels the Tree in an upward fashion and then descends once more to Malkuth, where we receive the end results. This is the meaning behind the word *karma* and the phrase, *reap what you sow*. Macrocosmically, it is associated with the Earth. Microcosmically, it is associated with the feet and the anus. Malkuth's colors are citrine, russet, olive, and black.

Summary

Understanding the mechanics of your interior spaces provides a good foundation for practical application. As you move forward into Chapter 6, and into the world of magic, remain open to any spiritual epiphanies, illuminations, and psychic experiences. Apply what you have learned thus far and do not be frightened that you are doing a particular magical operation incorrectly. Just like any recipe, if you follow it too closely, it never comes out the way you would like. "Use your intuition,"

"Do not become frustrated if you fail the first time," and "You are always right where you are supposed to be" are some words of advice that I wish I had heard early on in my magical journey. With that in mind, turn the page and take the next step in evolving magically and using your new magical wisdom as learned through Dragonflame.

Helix of Power

CHAPTER 6

RITUALS OF TRANSFORMATION

Each of the rituals of transformation in this chapter is the result of a personal spiritual experience. They have each been inspired by either clairvoyant visions or spontaneous out-of-body experiences (commonly known as astral travel). Because each ritual was given birth out of a necessity—sometimes one that I did not even know that I had—their DNA, so to speak, has been encoded with superior survival skills, ready now to be passed along to you.

Based on Sephiroth 4 through 10, the rituals are constructed to use harmonious, life-changing energies from the Practical Qabalah. The general structure of each ritual is as follows:

1. GPS (Goal, Purpose, Sacrifice)

2. Supplies

3. Duration

4. Offerings

5. Willpower List

6. God or Goddess

7. Further Explanations

8. Spell and/or Creative Visualization

9. Enhancements for the Advanced Student

All rituals demand the utmost attention and respect. Once their energies are put into motion, they will have far-reaching consequences and yield deep spiritual transformation. Whether you choose to perform one, two, or all the rituals in this chapter, the Dragonflame philosophy and talisman will guide you along the path of transformation in an organized and safe fashion. The experience unfolds in astounding and oftentimes unexpected ways.

Following these three simple steps will help add success and safety to your ritual of choice:

1. **Knowledge/understanding.** Before performing your chosen ritual, read its outline in its entirety. If there are any words you do not understand, be sure to check the Glossary on page 231 or do further research on your own. (I have added a References section and a Recommended Reading section on page 243 as well. Many of these books will discuss magic and philosophy in detail.) You may even want to read over the chosen ritual for three or four consecutive days, contemplating its meaning and mechanics. In this way, the ritual begins

to adapt to your personality and may even allude to a deeper purpose.

2. **Health.** Magic requires health. If you do not eat quality foods, maintain a well-balanced diet, drink fresh fruit and vegetable juices, and/or exercise regularly, try to do so for at least one week prior to beginning a ritual. Also be sure that you are well-rested. If you become ill during the ritual, stop. Wait until you recover fully and then start from the beginning.

3. **Visualization.** It is also helpful to first imagine yourself performing the ritual. Put on peaceful music and sit comfortably while visualizing yourself performing the chosen ritual in every detail. This will give you a better sense of rhythm, confidence, and security. Once you have prepared yourself, you are ready to begin.

"Come Back Done" Ritual (To Recover From Tragedy)

Forgive yourself for not being at peace. The moment you completely accept your non-peace, your non-peace becomes transmuted into peace.

—Eckhart Tolle, *The Power of Now: A Guide to Spiritual Enlightenment*

Goal: To recover from tragedy. (This can be an emotional, mental, and/or physical loss, on any level, from mild to severe.)

Purpose: So that I may enjoy life to its fullest.

Sacrifice: Earth Consciousness.

The sacrifice of being more earth-conscious is very profound. It means holding awareness of Earth's life force and how you interact with it. Mother Earth allows us to live and to walk on her surface, not the other way around. In honor of the Earth, try to be more conscious of everything you throw away, how you may be affecting the Earth's environment (for good or bad), and what it means to live a natural life.

Supplies: Dragonflame talisman (can be worn or placed on altar—see *Day 1*); black pillar candle; white pillar candle; 100-percent essential eucalyptus oil; 100-percent essential oil or incense of patchouli, rose, and sandalwood; brown cloth (to be used as an altar cloth); 24 stones (see the breakdown under *Day 2*); pictures and/or memorabilia of your favorite ancestors (see *Day 5*); natural offerings for your ancestors (see *Day 6*).

Duration: 10 Days. (The number 10 is associated with Mother Earth in the Practical Qabalah. The planet Earth symbolizes discernment, stability, silence, and wealth. The element of earth allows all other elements—air, water, and fire—to reside within it.)

Offering: You will be burning the following mixture of essential oils on *Day 10* and using it to bless your candles:

* ❋ 2 drops of rose
* ❋ 3 drops of sandalwood
* ❋ 5 drops of patchouli

Place the drops of oil directly into your oil diffuser to the Goddess Eithinoha (see the following section) on *Day 10* of your Willpower List or directly onto your candle for blessing. You may replace the oils with rose, sandalwood, and patchouli incense if you burn them simultaneously. To bless your candles with the incense, simply pass them through the smoke three times each.

Eithinoha: Native American Goddess of the Earth

Eithinoha (pronounced ay-thin-OH-ha) is the Iroquois Goddess of the Earth. Her energy is in perfect sync with the universe. When we walk in unison with her, she teaches us to catch the Earth's rhythm, and everything falls into place. In the Iroquois Indian language her name means *"Our Mother."* Eithinoha watches over all her children and asks only that we respect her realm, the Earth, and its environment. By leading a natural life and accepting who we are, we can change our lives for the better and receive her blessings.

The powerful archangel Uriel is also associated with the Earth realm. Uriel and Eithinoha's energies are similar in that they both lead to spiritual evolution as well as regeneration on all levels—physical, mental, emotional, and spiritual.

In this ritual you will be turning to Eithinoha to restore all that has come undone in your life. Remain humble and ask her to walk in front so that she may lead.

Medicine Wheel: Medication for the Soul

The early Native Americans understood that their lives depended on knowledge of the Earth, such as its herbs and sacred cycles. Spiritual leaders of the tribes used this knowledge in conjunction with esoteric practices for healing purposes. Their wisdom told them to work from the inside out and aim the healing energy at the soul of the person first, where the root cause lies. Learning by their example, one of the best and most potent ways for us to follow in their footsteps is by using the Native American Medicine Wheel.

The Native American culture understood the power of the wheel or circle. You don't have to search hard for this evidence.

Various-sized circles made by laying stones in a pattern on the ground can be found throughout North America and especially in Montana, Wyoming, Alberta (Canada), and parts of North and South Dakota. Some of the circles are hundreds, if not thousands of years old. Often, they would have a central point with spokes extending to the perimeter, resembling a wheel—thus the name Medicine Wheel. One of the most famous of these formations is found in Wyoming at the top of Bighorn Mountain Range. There are many theories for their existence, ranging from astrological and religious functions to Stonehenge-like calendars. One thing is certain: they are sacred structures and are recognized as such by the Native Americans as well as spiritualists worldwide.

The Medicine Wheel represents humanity as a whole in harmony with the cycles of Earth, Nature, and the universe. When we experience a loss or ailment in our lives, a part of this wheel has come undone or broken apart. It is up to us to ask for help repairing it. But how do we go about doing this? Well, you've heard of the saying "Mother knows best," haven't you? In this case, that is some of the best advice you can follow—let Mother Earth repair it for you.

The "Come Back Done" ritual is based on the concept of the Medicine Wheel and will help you turn to Mother Earth for help.

Willpower List

Day 1: Prepare Your Altar

❋ Begin by cleaning your altar with a mixture of 1 cup of spring water and 3 drops of 100-percent essential eucalyptus oil.

❋ Cover it with a brown cloth, preferably of cotton.

* Bless the black pillar candle with the rose/sandalwood/ patchouli mixture and place it on the far left corner of the altar.

* Bless the white pillar candle with the same oil mixture and place it on the far right corner.

* Obtain a statue or picture that you feel best represents Mother Earth or the goddess Eithinoha and place it between the pillar candles. If you choose not to wear the Dragonflame talisman place it in front of Eithinoha's picture.

* Sit quietly in front of your altar and feel the cleanliness you have created. Sense your altar's aura. Realize that the healing process has already begun.

Day 2: Choose 24 Stones, Minerals, or Crystals That Fascinate You

Today you will be choosing and researching different stones, not collecting or purchasing them. At the end of *Day 2* you will have a list of all 24 stones, minerals, or crystals (and a general idea of what they symbolize) that you will take with you on *Day 3* in order to collect or purchase them. All 24 stones will be used to make your Medicine Wheel, so you will need to break them down as follows:

* 1 citrine—to be placed at the eastern compass point on the altar to represent the element of air.

* 1 lapis lazuli—to be placed at the western compass point to represent the element of water.

* 1 garnet or rough ruby (which I prefer)—to be placed at the southern compass point to represent the element of fire.

* 1 black tourmaline—to be placed at the northern compass point to represent the element of earth.

* 1 clear quartz—to be placed at the center of the altar to represent Spirit.

* 12 stones, minerals, or crystals of your choice to represent the 12 calendar months of the year and the 12 zodiac signs. (They can all be the same or each one different. As long as they are meaningful to you, they will work.) Here are a few astrological associations to guide you:

Astrological Sign	Associated Stone
Aries (March 21–April 19)	Herkimer diamond, bloodstone
Taurus (April 20–May 20)	Moss agate, aventurine
Gemini (May 21–June 20)	Rutilated quartz, peridot
Cancer (June 21–July 22)	Rose quartz, amber
Leo (July 23–August 22)	Tiger's eye, citrine
Virgo (August 23–September 22)	Agate, carnelian

Libra (September 23–October 22)	Jade, coral
Scorpio (October 23–November 21)	Serpentine, opal
Sagittarius (November 22–December 21)	Turquoise, chrysocolla
Capricorn (December 22–January 19)	Garnet, Apache tear
Aquarius (January 20–February 18)	Amethyst, aquamarine
Pisces (February 19–March 20)	Fluorite, blue lace agate

❉ 7 stones, minerals, or crystals of your choice to represent the seven ancient planets: moon, sun, Saturn, Mars, Jupiter, Venus, and Mercury. (These can also all be the same or each one different. All that matters is that you feel an affinity for each one of them.) Here are some suggestions based on the Practical Qabalah:

Moon—Moonstone

Sun—Gold (pyrite or citrine can be used as well)

Saturn—Lead

Mars—Iron

Jupiter—Tin

Venus—Copper

Mercury—Brass

Whatever stones you choose, *Day 2* is about researching their magical and holistic properties. The number-one rule is that they must be 100-percent natural and from the Earth. You can choose elaborate ones that you will have to hunt for, or you may decide that on *Day 3* you will choose the majority of your stones while taking a long walk outside. Either way, find enjoyment in the process.

Day 3: Collect All Your Stones, Minerals, and/or Crystals

Go on a walk outside or on an outing to a local New Age store or rock shop and track down the stones you researched on *Day 2*. Collect and/or purchase them all.

Day 4: Day of Cleansing

Following the GPS of this ritual and the cleansing instructions given on page 127, cleanse and consecrate all of your stones. When you are finished, place them on a round plate and set it on the center of your altar. Don't worry about arranging the stones in any particular order for now; that comes later in the ritual. Cover them with a white cloth (silk is best) until you perform the rite on *Day 10*.

Day 5: Collect Images and Memorabilia of Your Ancestors

Spirits of family members, friends, and those held in reverence have long been called upon for help by the living in almost every culture. This custom, called *ancestor worship*, is still commonly practiced all around the world. Native American sha-mans call upon the spirits of the elders for guidance, Buddhists burn incense to the spirits of their family members for help and support, and many Christians and Roman Catholics bring flow-ers to lay in front of their loved ones' tombstones to keep their memories alive and to visit with their spirits. In this ritual, you will be praying to your ancestors to come to your aid.

Day 5 is about establishing a relationship with your an-cestors. Choosing ancestors that you feel an affinity toward or would like to have preside over your ritual is a great way to be-gin. You may have a grandmother you were particularly close to, or a friend's spirit you feel would add great power to your rite if called upon. Or perhaps you know an ancestor only through a story that has found its way down the family tree or through an old photo. Whatever the case, you will find that the ancestors have actually chosen you, not the other way around.

As you go about finding photos, statues, or anything they left behind, do it with the intent of reconnecting with their spirit and essence. Go about it in a humble manner. Remember, they are not held in captivity by the physical body any longer and therefore greatly outshine your intelligence and wisdom. Anything that reminds you of them will help attract their pres-ence. Place as many of these items as you like on your altar (as long as they fit) on either side of the plate of stones.

This particular Willpower assignment is a rite within itself and has a profound and cathartic effect on the soul. You may even dream of one of your ancestral spirits long after this rite is over. Once you reconnect, they will be there whenever you need their support.

Day 6: Collect Offerings for Your Ancestors

Today you will be collecting offerings for your ancestors. Some examples are flowers, herbs, crystals, food, a small bowl filled with sugar or grain, and aromatic resins and/or incense. During the rite on *Day 10* remember to light the resins and/or incense if you choose to use any. Place all your offerings on the altar any way you like. You can put them in front of or between different pictures of ancestors. Be creative and make the altar feel good to you.

At the end of the ritual you have the option of either burning all the offerings in a fire pit or simply throwing them back to Mother Earth. The offerings should be completely natural—nothing man-made.

Day 7: Solarize Your Soul

Stand outside at sunrise and again at high noon. Face the sun (do not look directly at it). Become aware of how a circle symbolizes the sun, moon, and Earth. Become aware of how Mother Earth has perfectly distanced herself from the sun in order to ensure the existence of life on her surface. As you think of how she receives his rays, begin to feel connected to the Earth's surface. Imagine yourself taking root once again in your mother as the plants, flowers, and trees do. Let her nourish you. Thank Mother Earth and the sun for their support.

Day 8: Lunarize Your Soul

Stand outside at sunset and again at midnight. Face the moon if you can see it. Become aware of how a circle symbolizes the sun, moon, and Earth. Become aware of how the moon works in conjunction with Mother Earth. As you think of her influence over the tides and our subconscious minds, ask yourself if the moon was once part of the Earth. Try to imagine the first humans to walk the Earth, your ancestors, who also looked up at the moon in wonder. Thank Mother Earth and the moon for allowing you to have this experience.

Day 9: Ground Your Self

Commune with Mother Earth. Become aware of how a circle symbolizes the sun, moon, and Earth. Take as long a walk as you can outdoors alone. This could be a park, cemetery, or walking path. As long as it is outside it will fulfill this particular Willpower task. The goal here is to reconnect your Spirit with Mother Earth and clear your mind of worries. With each step you take on your walk try to be aware of the earth beneath you. Think of the elements: natural spring water, the summer sun, the air you breathe, and the presence of Spirit manifesting in a vision of a rainbow. Become aware of the cycle of oxygen flowing into you, carbon monoxide flowing out and into the plants, and then oxygen flowing from them back into the air you breathe. Become aware that we are living on a Medicine Wheel—Mother Earth.

In preparation for your rite tomorrow try to hold the image of Eithinoha in your mind's eye as you slowly chant over and over as you fall asleep:

What was undone must now come back done.

Day 10: Spin the Wheel

Perform the ritual as outlined in the next section. When you are finished, celebrate by cooking an organic, all-vegetable meal. Share it with a friend or family member.

Mother Earth: The Rite (Day 10)

1. Put up a magic circle (optional, but recommended).

2. Sit in front of your altar.

3. Light the oil diffuser or incense.

4. Enter a relaxed state.

5. Ask your Higher Self to guide you and your Ancestral Spirits to support you.

6. Read the Creative Visualization and make your Medicine Wheel.

7. Sit in quiet meditation. Remain open to receive any spiritual messages.

8. Release and thank Goddess Eithinoha, Uriel, and the spirits.

9. Take down the magic circle if you have put one up.

10. Either throw all the offerings (they must be natural and therefore biodegradable) back to Mother Earth or burn them in an appropriate fire pit. You may opt to keep your Medicine Wheel on your altar for a few days, move it to another location, or dismantle it and keep it in a silk bag for later use.

Creative Visualization

Some years ago, it seemed that everything around me had come undone. I was in pain from a broken heart, there were financial troubles around me, and my loved ones were suffering emotionally. One night, I summoned my strength and prayed for a miracle. I willed my astral body to be free and to be receptive to Spirit. That night I received an answer. The following is what I experienced as I left my body and became aware I was on the astral plane. It is also your creative visualization and the core of this ritual. As you read it, really put yourself there. Experience the smells, sounds, and feelings. Build the images around you and allow yourself to spiritually emote.

I am standing in the middle of a lush green plateau, high on a hill. It is a clear, crisp day, not very windy. My attention is focused on a middle-aged lady walking about 10 feet in front of me. The first word I think of to describe her is natural. *I feel that we are somehow related. She has long, black hair and wears a simple white tunic. At first, this contrast of black and white strikes me as severe. Then I realize they are the symbols of heaven and earth, yin and yang.*

Now a maternal energy begins to emanate from her, letting me know she is aware of my presence within her realm. It speaks of hope and smells like a mixture of patchouli and wood burning in a fireplace on a fall night. The softest wind chimes ring in my soul, through my body. I am so calm. I allow my being to be taken over by an intense peace and I no longer care about anything. Not even those closest to me. I can see now that as she walks she creates a path for me. I follow her footsteps in hypnotic slow motion. We are in perfect synchronicity. I have become one with her movements, her vibrations.

Now she looks back at me over her shoulder. I see her profile and her gentle smile. She whispers, "What has come undone, must now come back done." The words make my solar plexus gush with an overwhelming emotion of gratitude, of love. And I think, Yes, yes, make it happen, make it all better. *She beckons me to chant with her. "What has come undone must now come back done. What has come undone must now come back done. What has come undone must now come back done." Together, we are whispering these words in a rhythm that matches our gait. And her hair, her long, Indian-black hair, begins to re-ravel itself magically up her back, following her spine. Slowly, it too is coming back done. My eyes follow the movement to the top of her head. It molds into a neat bun which is held tightly together with one long chopstick. And then, with all the power in me, I call out to all that must come back done, "Love, Health, Abundance, Balance!"*

How to Create Your Medicine Wheel

This is where the magic takes place. As you make your Wheel you are symbolically bringing all that was undone back done again. Conjure a feeling of spiritual wholeness and healing as you position your stones in the following manner:

Creation starts with a bang, so begin by placing the clear quartz in the very center of the plate to represent Spirit. Go about doing this with the consciousness of creating a big bang as the quartz touches the plate. After it's in place, put your hands over it and vibrate *Adonai Ha Aretz* (pronounced AH-dough-nie ha ah-RETZ). This is the god name associated with the Earth in the Practical Qabalah. It translates from Hebrew roughly as "lord of the earth."

Next, place the seven stones representing the ancient planets and your microcosmic body in a circle around the Spirit stone. As you do this, you are resetting the rhythm of your own personal universe, much as cardiologists do when they reset the rhythm of a heart through electrical impulse. When the stones are in place, put your hands over them and reestablish your wholeness by vibrating the Goddess's name and Archangel's name associated with the Earth: Eithinoha (pronounced ay-thin-OH-ha), and Uriel (pronounced OR-ree-el).

Now you are calling on the guardians of the four directions for guidance, protection, and counsel as you create the outer-most circumference of the wheel. Place the citrine in the east, garnet in the south, lapis lazuli in the west, and black tourmaline in the north. Put them at 12, 3, 6 and 9 o'clock, respectively, just as if the plate you are putting them on were a clock. Put your hands over them and call upon the choir of angels associated with the Earth known as the "fiery ones": Ashim (pronounced a-SHEEM).

Finally, out of the 12 stones representing the zodiac and calendar months, place three between each of the four directional stones to complete the outer circle and Medicine Wheel, thus creating harmony and balance within the Earth realm. Again, put your hands over them and vibrate: Malkuth (pronounced MAL-koot). This word means "kingdom" in Hebrew and refers to the kingdom of Earth.

Now, place your hands over the entire Medicine Wheel and thank Eithinoha in advance for giving you a second chance and leading you to a new path of harmony and healing. Honor her magic with a newfound respect for the elements and the environment they create.

Enhancements for the Advanced Student

* Before you begin the visualization, intone/vibrate *Adonai Ha Aretz*, *Eithinoha*, *Uriel*, *Ashim*, and *Malkuth*.

HOLY NAME	EXPLANATION
Adonai Ha Aretz	God Name
Eithinoha	Goddess Name
Uriel	Archangel
Ashim	Choir of Angels
Malkuth	Sephirah (sacred emanation)

* Begin your Willpower List so that *Day 10* falls on a full moon or Mabon.
* Perform *Day 10* on a Saturday at sunrise.
* Perform *Day 10* during the planetary hour of Saturn.

Moon Rite (To Open Your Mind's Eye)

The Road was lit with Moon and star -
The Trees were bright and still -
Descried I - by the distant Light
A Traveller on a Hill -
—Emily Dickinson

Goal: Open your mind's eye
Purpose: To develop psychic ability
Sacrifice: Vows to the Goddess

Supplies: Dragonflame talisman (can be worn or placed on altar), 1 deep purple taper candle, 1 moonstone, 100-percent essential jasmine oil.

Duration: 9 Days. (The number 9 is associated with the moon in the Practical Qabalah. It symbolizes strength, reproduction, and psychic energy.)

Offering: Burn jasmine oil in an oil diffuser each day of the ritual to Kuan Yin. (She is discussed in the next section.)

Kuan Yin: Chinese Goddess of Compassion

Once a month, ripe with psychic energy, the moon grows to her zenith. Blazing full with the sun's rays through the night sky, it is with great compassion and love for her children that she luminesces. Kuan Yin, the Chinese goddess of mercy and compassion, best encompasses the energies of the full moon for this ritual.

Throughout East and Southeast Asia, Kuan Yin, also known as Guanyin and as Kannon in Japan, has been worshiped for her deep compassion and mercy. Likened to the Christian goddess Mary, mother of Jesus, her followers pray to her to relieve suffering.

While our mind's eye remains closed we are asleep, or, in other words, not spiritually or psychically aware. In this state we inflict suffering not only on those who are awake but on ourselves as well. It is through this ritual that we are able to call on Kuan Yin's mercy to open our mind's eye so that we may take part in the psychic gifts that lie within and ultimately help relieve suffering.

Gifts of the Goddess

Through the doorway of the mind's eye lies our inner temple. It is a long walk to this temple, but once the doors are open and you take the first steps, certain abilities may be obtained, such as tranquility, wisdom, intuition, clairvoyance, guidance, magic, and love.

In order to use and perfect these gifts they must be shared. In order to share them, you must willingly become a tool of the Goddess. This entails taking marriage vows with her—for you are entering into a lifelong relationship with the Goddess when you finally open your mind's eye and heart's ear.

In any relationship, each partner gives an oath of togetherness, expressing their love for one another, and magic is no different. I took the traditional vows from the Book of Common Prayer and changed them a little to fit the needs of this ritual. I chose the traditional vows as a foundation for the new ones based on their profound simplicity and because they have been a part of the collective consciousness since the 16th century.

Who Is the Goddess?

You must first know who the Goddess is in order to make an oath and vow to her. No one can completely or properly describe who or what the Goddess is or means. Her energy is abstract and expressed through individuality. The one common denominator, however, is female energy, or *anima*.

The Goddess is the macrocosmic and microcosmic anima, as put in place by Creator. Her existence became necessary in order to give form to Creator's thoughts and therefore ours as well. Because she is considered the giver of form, her presence in the collective consciousness is one of severity. Any form given birth into the material realm becomes subject to time and doomed to the cycles of life and death, or birth, death, and, ultimately rebirth onto another plane of existence. In this way, she was allotted the archetypes of maiden, mother, and crone and became associated with the three cycles of the moon: new, full, and dark. Through her kinship with the moon we can also connect her with the subconscious mind.

The Goddess connects us to our subconscious mind through intuition. If you think of the subconscious mind as a person, your intuition would spring to life and begin speaking to you in nonverbal images, through dreams and sentient feelings. With practice, this may even occur in normal waking hours. The Goddess also teaches us that our intuition and her energy bring us closer to Creator.

By taking a vow to her, you are able to truly worship Creator fully. This is evident through her opposite and equally important energy, the God or masculine energy/animus as put into place by Creator. The anima and animus are two separate archetypes, yet they are in union. Think of a coin: two symbols embossed on the same metal. So when you take a vow to the Goddess, you are actually taking a vow to the God and ultimately Creator as well.

I believe we serve only one God (used in the generic sense) whose name is ineffable and whom I choose to call Creator. Creator is incomprehensible to us, neither male nor female, nothing and everything, the beginning and the end. There is no way to conceptualize who or what Creator is or looks like. Usually, the closest we get to this is the image of a kind and just king, mature, with a white beard, Zeus-like in appearance. Another image associated with Creator might be that of white light.

Once in a lucid dream I experienced Creator as white light emanating from a blazing white star, burning powerfully. As I became lucid I realized that I was floating in outer space. It was calm and peaceful. My point of focus was this pure white star not far off in the distance. I felt intense heat emanating from it. The star held me in perfect distance from it in order to be purified by its heat but not burned. I felt suddenly as if I could choose to move closer and intensify the purification process, but I chose not to. I knew that if I moved any closer I would be totally consumed by the white fire and would not be able to go back to my physical body (as a side note, to anyone familiar with pathworking this was my experience with the path of the High Priestess). This was the closest I have come to experiencing or comprehending Creator so far.

In order to further grasp this enigma, it is necessary to turn to all which It (for lack of a better term) has manifested—the entire cosmos, anything we can see, think, dream, or imagine, all of which is incorporated in the tarot. Once we do this, we can begin to realize the multitude of diverse paths from which to choose that can lead us back to Creator. Know the artist through the artist's works. And there are many. The Goddess is just one of them.

By taking a vow to her you are choosing to worship and serve Creator through your own spiritual experiences as received through the Goddess.

And remember, "the Goddess" is a deceptive title because it alludes to the feminine only. It encompasses not only the female aspect of ourselves and the universe, but the male as well—for within the Goddess can be found all the Gods.

Worshipping the Goddess

Worshipping, or giving honor to the Goddess is simple. Think of her as a young sister, a loving mother, and a wise grandmother. Respect your sister's innocence, don't do anything your mother would not approve of, and abide by your grandmother's advice.

Now think of Her as the new, full, and dark moon. On the new moon, do magic for love, money, starting new projects, knowledge, and/or giving birth to new ideas. On the full moon, do magic for love, sex, pleasure, fertility, success, health, power, and/or bringing goals to fruition. On the dark moon, do magic for protection, courage, removing obstacles, and/or getting rid of any unwanted influences.

Finally, think of Her as warrior, guide, and teacher. Keep yourself fit and disciplined so you too can be a spiritual warrior. Humble yourself so your ego doesn't block the correct path. Study, practice your magic, and listen to your inner voice so you can absorb all that you are taught. Knowledge is power.

If you remember these simple examples, then you will be following the advice of the great mystery schools when they say "enflame yourself with prayer."

On this note, read through the spell you will be using later in this ritual (*Moon's glow, diffuse light / Seal rendered to third sight / Aperite, Revelamini statim / Mind's eye, fire ignite / Future visions reveal tonight*) and write down what you feel it means. How does it touch you? What do you want it to mean? There is no right or wrong answer (see *Willpower Day 3*).

Willpower List

Day 1

If medically possible, cleanse your system by doing a liquid fast of only water and jasmine tea from midnight to 11:59 p.m. (Always consult your doctor before going on a fast.) If this is not possible, then go on a special one-day diet to help detoxify your system. Make a trip to the local health store and ask the employees for suggestions. Keep it all-natural. Remember to plan this in advance so that you may consult your doctor.

Day 2

Find and consecrate a moonstone using the GPS for this ritual.

Day 3

Analyze the spell used in this ritual. See *Worshipping the Goddess* on page 165.

Day 4

Procure an image or statue of Kuan Yin to place on your altar.

Day 5

Purchase a guided meditation CD and use it today.

Day 6

Follow the guided meditation CD.

Day 7

Follow the guided meditation CD.

Day 8

Follow the guided meditation CD.

Day 9

Follow the guided meditation CD.

Luna Lux Lucis: The Moonlight Spell

Moon's glow, diffuse light

Seal rendered to third sight

Aperite, Revelamini statim

Mind's eye, fire ignite

Future visions reveal tonight

Breaking the Seal

As Kuan Yin, the moon reveals herself as our compassionate and loving mother. This ritual will allow you to acknowledge that the moon we see with our physical eyes is an outer reflection of its spiritual counterpart within.

On the night of the full moon go outside and look up to the heavens. Focus your gaze on the moon and take in several deep breaths as you prepare to illuminate the mind's eye with the magical energy of the full moon. Imagine that you are breathing in the moon's silver rays. Begin to relax. You can sit or stand, whichever is more comfortable or appropriate.

Extend your arms toward the full moon and capture her energies by making a triangle with your fingers (connect your forefingers and thumbs). The moon will be in the center of your triangle.

Vibrate the following names of power: *Shaddai El Chai*, *Kuan Yin*, *Gabriel*, *Kerubim*, and *Yesod*.

GOD NAME	EXPLANATION
Shaddai El Chai	Loosely translates from Hebrew to mean the "Almighty Living God."
Kuan Yin	Chinese goddess of mercy and compassion.
Gabriel	Archangel of Yesod, the moon, the west, and of water. This angel's name means "Strength of God."
Kerubim	Choir of angels associated with Yesod and the moon. Their name means "The Strong Ones."
Yesod	Loosely translates from Hebrew to mean "Foundation."

Now, enflame your heart with the desire to evolve, to become more spiritual, and to tap into the full moon's powers. Then, with all your inner strength, courage, and conviction, say,

Kuan Yin, break the seal of my mind's eye. Open it now Great Mother. I am ready.

Still holding your triangle, fix your stare on the moon for a slow count of five seconds and then close your eyes. You will see an after-image on your closed eyelids. Imagine this image as clearly as possible, getting larger, coming towards you.

Chant the spell three, six, or nine times with your eyes closed (you'll have to commit it to memory). Then open them.

While you are chanting the spell, try to keep your mind as open and as still as possible. Lull yourself into a trance and remain receptive to the moon's energies. To help with this, visualize the moon's light as if it were fluorescent silver water flowing through you, entering through your mind's eye.

The full moon is a chalice tilting toward you, carefully pouring lustral waters forth from the heavens directly into your mind's eye. Feel them flow through your entire body, cooling each part as they pass down your throat and neck, chest, solar plexus, and down into your navel chakra (located about three inches or so below your belly button), where they collect in a pool of power.

When you are finished, take your moonstone (make sure it has been consecrated using the GPS for this ritual—see *Willpower Day 2*), kiss it once, ask the moon to shower you with her blessings, and hold it up to her as you say your vows:

> *Great Goddess, I choose to be your willing tool, with harm to none and for the greatest good of all, from this day forward, for better or for worse, for richer or for poorer, in sickness and in health, to love and to cherish, 'til death do us unite.*

Put your hands down. You are finished. Thank the moon with all your heart and ask her to bless you with luminous dreams.

Altar Arrangements and Instructions

Because all of your work is going into the Willpower List and so you can focus all your energies on opening your mind's eye, I've kept the altar setup uncomplicated:

* ❋ Place the image/statue of Kuan Yin at the back and center of the altar.

* ❋ Place the Dragonflame talisman in front of Kuan Yin if you choose not to wear it.

* ❋ Place the purple candle at the center of the altar in front of the Dragonflame talisman.

* ❋ Place the jasmine oil offering at the lower left.

* ❋ Place the moonstone at the center in front of the purple taper.

Kuan Yin

Dragonflame Talisman

Purple Candle

Moonstone

Jasmine

Offering

---

1. Time the ritual so that the ninth day of the Willpower List falls on the full moon.

2. Complete all eight days of the Willpower List.

3. On the ninth day of the Willpower List bless the purple taper candle with jasmine oil using the GPS in this ritual.

4. Prepare your altar.

5. Put up a magic circle (optional, but recommended).

6. Light the oil diffuser.

7. Light the purple taper.

8. Enter a relaxed state.

9. Ask Kuan Yin to guide you.

10. Stand in front of your altar. Focus on the flame of the candle and try to empty your mind of thoughts.

11. Place your hands, right over left, over the moonstone and vibrate the holy names associated with Yesod (just one time for each name, as given under Enhancements for the Advanced Student). Imagine silver light pouring down through your head and out your palms into the moonstone as you do this.

12. Continue to send silver light into the moonstone and chant the spell exactly nine times.

13. Release and thank the spirits and Goddess Kuan Yin.

14. Take down the magic circle if you have put one up.

15. Allow the candle to go out naturally.

16. In the evening, take the moonstone and go outside under the full moon.

17. Follow the instructions under *Breaking the Seal*.

18. Sleep with the moonstone under your pillow or beside your bed.

Enhancements for the Advanced Student

* Before you begin the spell, intone/vibrate *Shaddai El Chai*, *Gabriel*, *Kerubim*, *Shelachel*, *Chasmodai*, *Yesod*, and *Levanah*.

HOLY NAME	EXPLANATION
Shaddai El Chai	God Name
Gabriel	Archangel
Kerubim	Choir of Angels
Shelachel	Intelligence of the Moon
Chashmodai	Spirit of the Moon
Yesod	Sephirah (sacred emanation)
Levanah	Mundane Chakra

* Perform during the planetary hour of the moon.
* Perform on a Monday or Saturday.
* Perform on a blue moon or lunar eclipse.
* Perform when the moon is in Sagittarius.
* Do not perform when the moon is in Scorpio.

SOS Ritual (For Help in a Desperate Situation)

There is a tide in the affairs of men, which taken at the flood, leads on to fortune. And we must take the current when it serves, or lose our ventures.

—William Shakespeare, *Julius Caesar*

Goal: Erase all my obstacles.

Purpose: So that I may receive help and guidance in a desperate situation.

Sacrifice: Forgive yourself for past mistakes (One way of forgiving yourself is by letting go of the past. Promise the Goddess Yemayah that you will do your best to leave the past behind so you can face the present with all your attention.)

Supplies: Dragonflame talisman. (can be worn or placed on altar), two light-blue votive candles, one orange votive, jasmine oil or incense, some sand (approximately half a cup), a stencil (any arts and crafts store will have both sand and a stencil), one round plate approximately 3 to 4 inches in diameter, two pieces of parchment paper, any color ink pen, and scissors.

Duration: 8 days. (The number 8 is associated with the planet Mercury in the Practical Qabalah. It symbolizes messages, sacred geometry and symbols, and pure logic.)

Offering: Burn jasmine oil in a diffuser, or jasmine incense, to Yemayah during your ritual each day. (100-percent essential jasmine oil is the best to use, but a less expensive version is also acceptable.)

Fill out your Willpower List on your own for this ritual in your magic journal. (Check the appendix for extra help and inspiration.)

About This Ritual

Just as all the other rituals and spells in this book did, this one came to me in a lucid dream. I was panicking over an important family and business situation. *It isn't horrible yet*, I thought, *...or maybe it is*. I was really in a catch-22, didn't know what decision to make, and truly felt that the tides were against me. So, realizing that I had to start somewhere, I buckled down and forced myself to think of a goal and put it in writing. After I did, this ritual followed a few days later. From there, things finally started to straighten out.

The active ingredient in this ritual uses English gematria to achieve the desired goal. *Gematria* is an intimidating word for a simple concept: you assign a numerical value to each letter in the alphabet so that you can add the total of a word or phrase and compare it to others based on the same sum. For example, this ritual uses the English gematria for the letters S-O-S. *S* is the 19th letter in the alphabet and *O* is the 15th. Therefore, 19-15-19 is the numerical substitute for S-O-S. Add all three letters together and you get 53. Here are some other words that total 53: *banish, soar, reign, womb*.

Using this concept, SOS takes on deeper meanings. For example:

* ✳ "Banish" the negative conditions.

* ✳ "Soar" above your problems.

* ✳ "Reign" over your worries.

* ✳ Be reborn by receiving life giving wisdom from the "womb" of the Goddess.

The Powerful Number 8

The powerful number 8 served as the building block and inspiration for this ritual in many different ways. Take a look at some of its hidden transformations:

∞

Lying on its side it creates the *lemniscate*, or infinity sign. The infinity sign represents Spirit, clear thought, and guidance from your Higher Self. It symbolizes that there is a timeless place that issues forth divine energy with which to create. During the ritual you will put the two letter *S*'s (**SOS**) together to create the infinity sign above the letter *O* (**SOS**) to symbolize Spirit flowing freely into your mind and heart.

Depending on how you take it apart, the number 8 can be used to create two letter *S*'s, one normal and the other in reverse. It can also be separated into two letter *O*'s.

For this ritual, the two letter *S*'s also double as symbols for the waves of the goddess Yemayah's great ocean. The letter *O* acts as a symbol for the head or mind. This will help you visualize your obstacles being cleared and help focus your intent.

The number 8 also happens to be the final result in our gematria:

SOS: 19 + 15 + 19 = 53; 5 + 3 = 8.

8 in English gematria means "the cure." How perfect is that for getting rid of obstacles?

The cure: 20 + 8 + 5 + 3 + 21 + 18 + 5 = 80; 8 + 0 = 8

Another way to understand the number 8's power is through the tarot. There are four number-8 cards in the minor arcana, one for each suit: wands, cups, swords, and pentacles. They have both positive and negative meanings we can learn from:

1. **Eight of Wands**—Positive. Communication, messages, swift answers. **Lesson:** Communicate with Spirit and ask for help. The ritual begins with the Eight of Wands. The moment you decided to do this ritual the Eight of Wands was activated, either consciously or subconsciously. Spirit's energy begins to pour forth and heal your emotional losses, represented by the Eight of Cups.

2. **Eight of Cups**—Negative. Abandonment, betrayal. **Lesson:** Life is change. Everything changes. Nothing stays the same. The past does not make you who you are. Move forward or be swallowed by the past. This is your sacrifice. Yemayah's one condition—that you let go of the past and face the present. Take time to mourn over your losses, but then move on. When you do, she will provide you with the courage to face and conquer the Eight of Swords.

3. **Eight of Swords**—Negative. A catch-22 situation. No answer in sight. **Lesson:** Without friction we would not evolve. In preparation for the ritual you will pour a thin layer of sand on the plate, which will be used to symbolize the letter *O* in the acronym SOS. Within the letter *O* you will draw eight swords using your finger in the sand. The eight swords symbolize your obstacles and problems. The act of drawing them takes your problems from the mind, where they are intangible, hiding, and ambiguous, and traps them in a place where you can confront them and consciously curse and counteract them. The sand also acts as a cleansing earth elemental and nullifies the problems by using the Eight of Disks.

4. **Eight of Disks**—Positive. Prudence, a call for organization. Also symbolizes a job or perhaps a place of work.
   Lesson: Do not be afraid to face the situation head-on.
   Accept it, face it, and resolve it through prudence and
   good judgment. Remember, facing your fears will give
   you more control over them.

Yemayah: African Goddess of the Ocean

Yemayah is an African goddess of the ocean. She is deeply
nurturing, in charge of the tides of life, and can be either calm or
destructive. She is associated with the moon in all of its phases.

In this ritual, you will be calling out to that aspect of
Yemayah at her most beneficent phase, the full moon, when
her sway over the tides is at its zenith. The plate with sand on
it represents the shore where your problems will be identified
and confronted. On the last day of your ritual, with the moon
at its fullest, Yemayah's high tide will erase all your obstacles as
her waves come crashing onto shore and wash away the writing
in the sand. You enact this by clearing the Eight of Swords from
the sand with your finger or athame.

Yemayah's colors are blue and orange for this ritual. These
complementary colors are also associated with the Sephirah
Hod and the element of water. *Hod*, the eighth sacred emanation found on the Qabalah, means "splendor" in Hebrew. It
represents pure mind and intellect. Hod can be better understood in comparison to its opposite Sephirah, Netzach, which
represents pure instinct and emotion and is associated with the
element of fire.

One of the symbols used in conjunction with Hod is the
downward-pointing triangle. It is used to represent the element

of water. It will be used in this ritual through the placement of the votive candles.

Altar Arrangements and Instructions

Day 1

Find a round plate approximately 3 to 4 inches in diameter. This plate will represent the letter *O*. Pour a thin layer of sand on it and place it on the altar.

Using the stencil and scissors cut two capital letter *S*'s out of parchment paper. They should be about 5 to 6 inches high depending on the size of the plate you have chosen.

Center the S's and the plate on the altar so they spell S-O-S. Remember, the plate is going to double as your letter *O*, so you will be putting an 'S' to the left of it and an 'S' to the right of it, not on the letter *O* plate.

Place the Dragonflame talisman back and center of the altar if you choose not to wear it. Bless all three votives (two blue and one orange) with jasmine oil using the GPS system. Center them on your altar above the SOS.

Place the offering in the lower left corner.

```
                    Dragonflame Talisman
        Blue Candle / Orange Candle / Blue Candle
                           SOS


    Oil Diffuser
```

1. Put up your magic circle (optional, but recommended).

2. Light the offering in the upper left corner of the altar.

3. Light the blue candle on the left and say, *Great Goddess Yemayah, help me identify and confront my problems.*

4. Using your index finger draw four slash marks to the right (/ / / /) and then four to the left (\ \ \ \) on top of them, making a cross-hatch figure to represent the Eight of Swords. As you do, imagine that you are identifying your problems and trapping them in the sand.

5. Do the visualization as outlined in the next section.

6. When you are finished with the visualization, take the orange votive and place it below the plate.

7. Take the letter *S* on the left, turn it 45 degrees to the right, and center it above the plate with the sand. It now represents one of Yemayah's waves and the lower half of the infinity sign. Place a blue votive on each side of it. (Your altar should now look like *Day 2*.)

8. Extinguish the candle. Thank and release the spirits and Yemayah.

9. Take down the magic circle if you have put one up.

Day 2

Dragonflame Talisman

Blue Candle, letter 'S' turned on its side, Blue Candle

OS

Orange Candle

Oil Diffuser

---

1. Put up your magic circle (optional, but recommended).

2. Light the offering in the upper left corner of the altar.

3. Light both blue candles, starting with the one on the left, and say, *Great Goddess Yemayah, grant me guidance, grant me that which I need that I do not even know to ask for.*

4. Do the visualization.

5. Take the letter *S* on the right, flip it upside down and turn it 45 degrees to the left. It now represents another of Yemayah's waves and the upper half of the infinity sign. Match it together with the first wave to create the infinity sign. Place a blue votive in the left loop of the newly created infinity sign and another in its right loop. (Your altar should now look like *Day 3.*)

6. Extinguish the candles, starting with the one on the right. Thank and release the spirits and Yemayah.

7. Take down the magic circle if you have put one up.

Day 3

Dragonflame Talisman

Blue Candle in left loop, Blue Candle in right loop

O

Orange Candle

Oil Diffuser

---

1. Put up your magic circle (optional, but recommended).

2. Light the offering in the upper left corner of the altar.

3. Light the orange candle, then the blue candle on the right, and then the one on the left. Say, *Great Goddess Yemayah, may your spirit pour through me and erase all my obstacles, like writing in the sand washed away by the sea.*

4. With your index finger or athame smooth out the sand, clearing away the Eight of Swords. Place the orange candle in the middle of the sand.

5. Do the visualization.

6. Thank and release the spirits and Yemayah.

7. Take down the magic circle if you have put one up.

8. Let the candles burn out naturally. Throw the sand back to Mother Earth.

Visualization

Imagine you are standing on the end of a short pier, which juts out into a calm, rhythmically moving, aquamarine ocean. The wind is gentle and warm. A light-blue sky, cloudless, allows the sun's rays to gently warm your skin. It is a perfect day, and it makes you feel calm. You are filled with hope. It's so perfect, and the elements are so harmonized, that you feel a sweet delirium. You are acutely aware of the sea and her tides. You are as one. She is the great unknown, the great mother, sacred Yemayah. Somehow, you have caught her attention. It is a blessing.

With all the power in you, from the depth of your soul, you call out in a loud voice, "Nineteen, fifteen, nineteen." You do this over and over. Your voice vibrates and echoes through the sky and travels to the ends of the universe. You send out this SOS and are certain that Yemayah hears you.

Now, you can see that every wave carries help. Their very movement is aiding you as they come towards you, advancing to the shore. Yemayah has answered you.

Finally, the tides have turned in your favor...you whisper with relief, "Thank you, thank you, thank you."

Enhancements for the Advanced Student

✴ Before you begin the visualization intone/vibrate *Elohim Tzaboath*, *Yemayah*, *Michael*, *Beni Elohim*, *Tiriel*, *Taphthartharath*, *Hod*, and *Kokab*.

HOLY NAME	EXPLANATION
Elohim Tzaboath	God Name
Yemayah	Goddess Name
Michael	Archangel
Beni Elohim	Choir of Angels
Tiriel	Intelligence of Mercury
Taphthartharath	Spirit of Mercury
Hod	Sephirah (sacred emanation)
Kokab	Mundane Chakra

* Perform when Mercury is direct.

* Perform on a Wednesday and/or when the moon is in Gemini.

* Perform during the planetary hour of Mercury.

Spiral Ritual (For Magical Progress and Development)

Beloved, gaze in thine own heart, the holy tree is growing there;

From joy the holy branches start, and all the trembling flowers they bear.

—William Butler Yeats, *The Two Trees*

Goal: Magical Progress and Development.

Purpose: To Know Myself Better.

Sacrifice: Patience. (Promise the archangel Michael that you will be more patient with yourself and others.)

Supplies: Dragonflame talisman (can be worn or placed on altar); 100-percent essential oil of frankincense, allspice, and ginger; 1 red taper candle; 1 oil diffuser.

Duration: 7 days. (The number 7 is associated with the planet Venus in the Practical Qabalah. It symbolizes the fire of transmutation, passion, love, will, change, and progress.)

Offering: Magical Development oil (see below) must be burned in an oil diffuser each day of the ritual to the Archangel

Michael. It will also be used to bless the candle you will be placing on the altar (see *Altar Arrangement*).

Magical Development Oil

3 drops of essential frankincense

3 drops of essential allspice

6 drops of essential ginger

Fill your diffuser with water and place all drops of oil directly into it at the time of the ritual. All drops of oil can go directly onto your candle as well when you are ready to bless it.

Frankincense is associated with the sun and the Higher Self; ginger, with the planet Mars, fire, and force; and allspice with motivation and the planet Uranus, which rules electricity and magic. The combination of all three will properly direct the planetary energies towards the goal of magical development.

Fill out your Willpower List on your own for this ritual in your magic journal. (Check the Appendix for extra help and inspiration.)

Purity of Intention

An important aspect of this ritual is knowing and understanding your motivation. Why do you want magical progress and development? If your answer is to obtain power, you are headed in the wrong direction. If it is to get closer to the Stone, you have answered correctly. There is a fundamental difference between the two. The former will lead you astray, and the latter will guide you flawlessly.

To ensure that your motivation stays pure, I have chosen the Archangel Michael to preside over this ritual—or, I should say, *he* chose. His energy rules the southern quadrant, high noon, the season of summer, the zodiacal sign of Leo, and the element of fire, all of which are sacred signs of power, strength, and transformation.

In Catholicism the standard representation of Archangel Michael depicts him with one foot on Satan's head. In the world of magic this can be interpreted as dominance over the lower astral realm or primal human desires. He stands with sword ready to strike the deathblow in his right hand and a scale in his left. The sword represents force and the magician's will. The scale represents truth, righteousness, and balance. So it is through these virtues that Michael brings magical progress and development.

One of the most mysterious facets of this ritual is the outcome. Even though you are working toward a particular goal, you may have no clue as to how it will manifest. Just as my spell states, each of us dances the spiral dance—and each in a very different way. Magic is a deeply individual and personal experience; thus, the results of this ritual will be personalized as well. Keep your intent pure by constant reference to Michael's virtues, and the outcome will be a step in the right direction instead of one forward and three back.

Visualization: There Is a Treasure

In my spell I make mention of a ladder. This is the famous Jacob's Ladder as found in the Book of Genesis. Jacob witnesses angels climbing a ladder from Earth to heaven in his vision. In this way, a ladder becomes more than just a mundane symbol for reaching that which we cannot usually reach. It takes on a much loftier magical definition of a connection point from one plane of existence to another—or from one state of consciousness to another. By reading the biblical passage and meditating on the imagery you can energize and awaken an otherwise dormant element and transform it into a conscious key to access your magical treasure house.

Enter a relaxed state and read the following passage from Genesis 28:12:

> *And [Jacob] dreamed, and behold a ladder set up on the earth, and the top of it reached to heaven: and behold the angels of God ascending and descending on it.*

Now, close your eyes and imagine yourself ascending a ladder to a higher realm. As you climb, there are angels on either side of you, heavenly helpers to protect you during your journey. Feel secure as you imagine yourself rising to another plane of existence. See yourself heading into a blazing white light where the Philosopher's Stone resides. Once you are at the top of the ladder and surrounded by the white light, say the following affirmation three times:

> *Now I choose to listen to my Higher Self.*

Climb back down the ladder slowly and ground yourself by snapping or clapping once, and say,

> *Wide awake!*

This is a simple technique to help your subconscious mind apply a magical association to the image of a ladder. The more you do this, the more it will give you control over that portion of your mind that is the doorway to the mysteries. Now, when you dream of a ladder, it will be your subconscious sending you an important message.

After Jacob had the vision of the ladder, he wrestled with an angel:

And Jacob was left alone; and there wrestled an...[angel] with him until the breaking of the day. And when he saw that he prevailed not against him, he touched the hollow of his thigh; and the hollow of Jacob's thigh was out of joint, as he wrestled with him. [Genesis 32:24–25]

The quest for magical progress and spiritual development is part of the same quest for the Treasure or Philosopher's Stone. The halls where it lies are protected by great sacrifice and purity, however, and one must wrestle with a seemingly supernatural force in order to get there. Wrestling with this force, or angel, is a metaphor for our inner wrestling to make the right decisions. This is a metaphor that can help us become aware of the natural friction that takes place on the Earth plane, where the illusion of time exists. It's when we are able to calm ourselves and go within through meditation and/or ritual that we are finally able to climb Jacob's Ladder and remove ourselves from time's captivity. Then the answers come to us and we learn from the friction that takes place within and without. This is when we become thankful to Mother Earth, for it is through her that we receive the necessary friction which eventually leads to the gold.

Altar Arrangements and Instructions

Simply place the Dragonflame talisman back and center of your altar if you choose not to wear it, one red taper candle in the middle, and your offering on the lower left corner.

```
+------------------------------------------------+
|                                                |
|                                                |
|              Dragonflame Talisman              |
|                  Red Candle                    |
|                                                |
|                                                |
|                                                |
| Offering                                       |
|                                                |
+------------------------------------------------+
```

Magical development is about concentration and focus, not elaborate preparations. Having one candle in the middle of the altar confidently directs the mind toward one goal. The color of the candle, red, evokes a bold, fiery energy, indicative of the path of spirituality.

As you place the candle on your altar remember that by performing this ritual, you willfully place yourself onto a path of solar activity. This means that illumination, new knowledge, and power will come to you. It also means that responsibility, death of old beliefs, and acceptance of new philosophies will be expected of you.

1. Prepare your altar.

2. Put up a magic circle (optional, but recommended).

3. Light the oil diffuser.

4. Light the red taper candle.

5. Enter a relaxed state.

6. Ask Archangel Michael to guide you.

7. Sit in lotus position in front of your altar. Focus on the flame of the candle and try to empty your mind of thoughts.

8. Chant the spell given in the next section for up to seven minutes.

9. Release and thank the spirits and Archangel Michael.

10. Take down the magic circle if you have put one up.

11. Extinguish the candle (remember to use a candle snuffer).

Spiral Dance Spell

Dance the Spiral Dance

Open Doors with Trance

Climb the Ladder Climb

Within World Sublime

Seek True Will Seek

Humble Ego Keep

Rise with Angels Rise

The Stone of the Wise

Enhancements for the Advanced Student

✳ Before you begin the incantation, intone/vibrate *YHVH Tzabaoth, Michael, Elohim, Hagiel, Kedemel, Netzach,* and *Nogah.*

HOLY NAME	EXPLANATION
YHVH Tzabaoth	God Name
Michael	Archangel
Elohim	Choir of Angels
Hagiel	Intelligence of Venus
Kedemel	Spirit of Venus
Netzach	Sephirah (sacred emanation)
Nogah	Mundane Chakra

* Perform during the waxing moon.

* Prepare it so the last day of your ritual coincides with the full moon (all the better if it also coincides with a Friday and/or when the moon is in Libra).

* Perform on the summer solstice.

* Perform on a full moon lunar eclipse or a new moon solar eclipse.

* Perform during the planetary hour of Venus.

* Sprinkle a small handful of mullein herb around the red candle before beginning the ritual. Mullein is associated with the element of fire and spiritual transformation. When you are finished with the ritual, throw the mullein back to Mother Earth.

Vesta Ritual (To Manifest Continued Success)

The most powerful weapon on earth is the human soul on fire.
—Ferdinand Foch

Witch's Wink: Don't be surprised if you find yourself in a leadership role after completing this one!

Goal: Continued success.

Purpose: So I may preserve the sacred flame.

Sacrifice: Truth. (The sacrifice of truth means to be more aware of its opposite: self-deception and lies. Promise the Goddess Vesta that you will be more truthful to yourself.)

Supplies: Dragonflame talisman (can be worn or placed on altar), a piece of white paper and pen to write your wish or goal on, 100-percent essential cinnamon oil, one black candle, one white candle, one large yellow or gold candle, fresh flowers, several acorns (you can substitute acorns with the bark of an oak tree, oak twigs, basil, or fennel).

Duration: 6 days (The number 6 is associated with the sun, considered a planet to the ancients, in the Practical Qabalah. It symbolizes balance, creativity, truth, the Higher Self, fame, and recognition. Its energies will help achieve a lasting goal that shines continuously like the rays of the sun.)

Offering: Burn cinnamon oil in a diffuser, or cinnamon incense if you prefer, to Vesta during your ritual each day.

Fill out your Willpower List on your own for this ritual in your magic journal. (Check the appendix for extra help and inspiration.)

About This Ritual

Through the goddess Vesta's help, this ritual will direct your soul's inner fire in the best possible way to manifest continued success for you, thus adding a higher level of quality to your life and freeing up your time to do more of what you love.

There are two types of fire utilized in this ritual: solar and elemental. The solar fire symbolizes the God Force or Great Abba. His rays of illumination heat you, creating spiritual fervor, and energize your astral body and aura with power, just as a rock holds heat in the evening after sitting in the afternoon sun. The elemental fire, represented by the burning pyre, symbolizes spiritual truth. The element of air needed to keep the fire burning represents knowledge and teaching.

Earth and water are also put into use, symbolized by sand and the ocean. The ocean symbolizes the Goddess Force or Great Amma. Her shore represents a place of psychic power, a place where two harmonious elements, earth and water, come into contact with one another. It is also an area where the No Trespassing law does not exist, representing a sacred, free area that answers to no one. The calming rhythm of her waves reach a neutral area where all are allowed to walk. The sand represents the earth element at its most receptive yet stable state. Walking along the shore is relaxing and feels good on the soles of our feet and has the power to remove negativity at the same time.

In this way, all five elements (earth, air, fire, water, Spirit—amma/abba) have been used to create a powerful ritual.

Vesta: Ancient Roman Goddess of the Hearth

Ancient Roman goddess of the hearth and home, Vesta represents sustenance and light. Her priestesses were called the Vestal Virgins because of a vow of chastity they took for 30 years. Part of their job was to make sure a fire lit to Vesta never went out. This was considered a spiritual fire symbolizing control, life, spirit, knowledge, truth, purity, and transformation.

Vesta held a very important status within Roman society, as she presided over the element of fire, which was safely contained and utilized in the hearth. She provided control over the fire, which gave warmth, cooked food, and also served divinatory and various spiritual purposes.

Call on Vesta to help bring and/or keep the family together, divine the future, provide purpose to material goals, instill leadership qualities, and enflame you with spiritual truths. She is a very serious goddess and her energy creates lasting and powerful change. She is most apt to help teachers and spiritual leaders, or those who aspire to be such.

Altar Arrangements and Instructions

Flowers

Black Candle   Dragonflame Talisman   White Candle

Yellow Candle

(Parchment Paper with Goals Under Yellow Candle)

Oil Diffuser

- Dress the black candle with virgin olive oil while saying, *I consecrate this candle to the Great Goddess.*

- Place it on the back left corner of the altar (from the perspective of facing your altar).

- Dress the white candle with virgin olive oil while saying, *I consecrate this candle to the Great God.*

- Place it on the back right corner of the altar, opposite the black candle.

- Place either your oil diffuser or incense on the front left corner. If you are using an oil diffuser put six drops of cinnamon oil in it.

- In the center of the altar place the yellow or gold candle dressed with cinnamon oil. This is your main candle. It holds your wish, so make sure you bless it with the goal and purpose I described, using the format I explained earlier in the book. Place the piece of parchment paper with your goal written on it under this candle. If you do not have a specific goal, simply write "Continued Success."

- Make a circle around the yellow wish candle with the acorns or one of the substitutes.

- Put the flowers in a vase and put them at the back of the altar in the center. These are an offering for Vesta as well.

- Place the Dragonflame talisman in front of the vase of flowers if you choose not to wear it.

Directions

Begin by writing your goal (if you do not have one, write "Continued Success") or what it is you want to achieve on the piece of parchment paper. For each day of the ritual you will:

1. Prepare your altar.

2. Put up a magic circle (optional, but recommended).

3. Light the oil diffuser or incense.

4. Light the white candle first.

5. Light the black candle second.

6. Light the yellow or gold candle last.

7. Enter a relaxed state.

8. Ask Vesta to guide you.

9. Begin the visualization.

10. Chant the spell.

11. Finish the visualization.

12. Release and thank the spirits and Vesta.

13. Take down the magic circle if you have put one up.

14. Extinguish the candles in reverse (remember to use a candle snuffer).

On the last day of the ritual you will follow this list again. The only difference will be that you will burn the paper with your goal on it using the flame of the yellow candle after you finish the visualization (step 11). Everything else will remain the same. After step 14, blow the ashes to the wind. You are finished. Now the important part is to relax and let go. Do not think about the ritual anymore or you will hinder it. Let the energy work for you in its own time.

Visualization

In this visualization, Vesta guides you to a lit pyre symbolizing the sacred fire of truth and knowledge, which serves as your beacon. Chant the spell as long as you like, but do so at least nine times. Stop chanting at the point in the visualization when you reach the pyre.

It is high noon between June 9 and June 15. You are in ancient Italy, near Rome, honoring Vesta at her yearly celebration called the Vestalia. You are walking along the seashore dressed in a white toga. It is the most beautiful day you can remember in a long time. It seems perfect. You are walking in a southerly direction toward the sun, and the waves of the ocean are lightly breaking to your right. There are many people behind you in a single file. They are following you. There is a fervent, serious tone to your voice as you sing, "Praise Vesta." Some distance in front of you and inland a bit, you see a fire burning. Instinctively you know this is where you must guide the others. This is where Vesta is guiding you. With perfect concentration you focus only on arriving at the fire. As you walk to it you begin chanting:

Spell of the Eternal Flame

Eternal Flame Burning Within

Golden Embered Coal

Perfect Success, Continued Success

Now For Every Goal

Roaring Fire, Image of Strength

Forever Rampant Abba

To the Pyre of Truth Let Me Guide All Who Seek
Along the Shores of Amma

You spiral to your left 180 degrees, as if following an arc that someone has drawn into the sand, and stop in front of the fire facing north. You realize this fire has always been here, taken care of by the Vestal Virgins. It had only been waiting for you to seek it out. All is quiet and you take a moment to feel the warmth of the sun above, the sound of the waves, the smell of the burning wood, the taste of the salt air, and the embrace of the sand below. See your goal as clearly as possible in front of you. When you see it strongly and when it feels right to you, release it into the flames to the Goddess Vesta. Know that you have succeeded already.

Enhancements for the Advanced Student

❋ Before you begin the spell intone/vibrate YHVH *Aloah V'Daath*, *Vesta*, *Raphael*, *Malachim*, *Nakhiel*, *Sorath*, *Tiphareth*, and *Sol*.

HOLY NAME	EXPLANATION
YHVH Aloah V'Daath	God Name
Vesta	Goddess Name
Raphael	Archangel

Malachim	Choir of Angels
Nakhiel	Intelligence of the Sun
Sorath	Spirit of the Sun
Tiphareth	Sephirah (sacred emanation)
Sol	Mundane Chakra

✻ Time the start day of your ritual so that the last day coincides with the full moon.

✻ Sprinkle the acorns (or whichever substitute you used) around your own hearth (or homemade fire) to invite Vesta's energy into your home. If you do not have a hearth, sprinkle them out your front door, back door, or both. If you live in an apartment complex, put them in a bowl and place it in the room you consider to be the heart of your house for three full days and nights. On the morning of the fourth day, throw them back to Mother Earth.

✻ Begin and end each of the first five days of the ritual with the LBRP and BRH. Perform the last day of the ritual with the Watchtower ritual (as described in *Modern Magik* by Donald Michael Kraig) or one comparable.

✻ Upon successful completion, reward yourself with a dinner out!

✻   ✻   ✻

Mars Ritual (Tapping Into Your Reservoir of Power)

I hope our wisdom will grow with our power, and teach us that the less we use our power the greater it will be.

—Thomas Jefferson

Goal: Power.

Purpose: Personal transformation.

Sacrifice: Perseverance. (Promise the god Mars that you will persevere as much as you can in order to obtain personal transformation and better serve Creator.)

Supplies: Dragonflame talisman (can be worn or placed on altar), 100-percent essential oil of ginger, Dragon's Blood resin, red taper candle, white taper candle, Florida Water or Hoyt's Cologne, and small cauldron or receptacle (in which to burn the Hoyt's Cologne or Florida Water).

Duration: 5 days. (The number 5 is associated with the planet Mars in the Practical Qabalah. It symbolizes strength, vigor, transformation and power.)

Offering: Burn ginger oil in an oil diffuser each day of the ritual to Mars. It will also be used to bless the candle. You can use allspice oil as a substitute.

Mars: Ancient Roman God of Power

As the son of Juno and Jupiter, Mars is a powerful and honored god in the Roman pantheon. He was worshipped as a god of war and power by all, including the Roman military. Interestingly, he was also considered a benevolent protector and a god of fertility.

Mars resides over Tuesday, and his energy is fiery, transformative, and aggressive. We can turn to him for protection, energy, courage, and power. He also helps us move forward when our efforts are feeling futile or stalled. Mars enters our life when we are ready to understand the opposite of defeat—victory—and when we ask for the power to discern the battles from the war.

In order to channel Mars's energy successfully, you must promise him that you will persevere more. When things are the most difficult, a true warrior and child of Mars struggles onward rather than giving up. This most coveted sacrifice of perseverance will catch Mars's attention and favor.

Geburah: The Essense of Power

There are many definitions of power, ranging from strength and force to influence over others and how well one controls one's environment. In magical philosophy these definitions are accepted and expanded by the belief that the actual essence of power is an energy that can be tapped into and manipulated safely and successfully.

The Practical Qabalah states that this essence can be found in the fifth Sephirah or sacred emanation called Geburah. When translated from Hebrew into English, *Geburah* means "severity," a harsh noun describing the possible consequences of using Geburah's energies. This Sephirah achieves its goals by breaking down or cutting away, as opposed to the Sephirah preceding it, Chesed, which builds up and fortifies (see the next ritual for Lakshmi/Ganesha).

A simple example would be food and diet. Chesed builds up the body with food. Geburah breaks down the fat and makes the body thinner through exercise and natural metabolism.

Another example, simple but thought-provoking, would be a spiral—Chesed being a spiral moving in a clockwise, or *deosil*, direction, and Geburah being a spiral moving in a counterclockwise, or *widdershins* direction. The clockwise spiral represents movement towards our goal, the crescendo aspect, and yang/masculine energy—the waxing moon. The counterclockwise spiral represents the necessary sacrifices to obtain the goal, the winding-down aspect, and yin/feminine energy—the waning moon. A natural balance takes place, parallel to nature, the world, and the cosmos as a whole.

The concept of breaking down happens on every level—spiritual, emotional, mental, and physical. It is happening at every moment. Even now, as you read this, time is passing and the physical body is aging, slowing down the rate at which it regenerates. Somewhere along your lifeline there will no longer exist a Chesed or building-up cycle, at which time the physical body will cease working and free the spirit from its material confines.

This severe aspect of Geburah is readily apparent in Nature's cycle of life. Take the simplest of examples: a lioness hunting for food. She spots the weakest prey and kills it in order to feed herself and her cubs. Her instinct for survival, just like evolution, is merciless. It is the strong that survive. In this way Geburah holds up to its meaning of severity. It is a necessary energy that always leaves room for new life and is mistakenly considered evil by some who lack understanding.

We are not to be afraid of this energy, however, but accepting of its aggressive potency that exists in the universe and within each one of us. By embracing and exploring this force through ritual we learn how to manipulate it to our benefit and experience life to its fullest. We also learn where our limitations are, and how strong or weak we are, and then go about adjusting ourselves accordingly. It is through this trial and error that we experience personal transformation, a byproduct of true power, and fulfill the purpose of this ritual.

The Three Virtues

As always, there are rules that must be followed in order to manage power without harming or destroying yourself or others. These can be found in the magical symbol attributed to Geburah: the sword. It is this same sword that bestows knighthood or beheads, depending on what resides in the soul and the destiny of the recipient.

The famous 20th-century British occultist and author Dion Fortune maintains that there are three virtues that will enable one to wield power properly: discipline, control, and stability. (See Dion Fortune, *The Mystical Qabalah*, York Beach, Maine: Samuel Weiser, 1984, p. 184.)

Discipline and control go hand in hand. The expert marksman practices until he has total control over his weapon. A black belt in martial arts disciplines him- or herself through proper diet to keep the body trim and healthy, through meditation to keep the mind calm and clear, and through repetitive movements for instant recall when needed—all with the goal of greater control.

An adept of the magical arts disciplines him- or herself much as the black belt does, with proper diet, meditation, and repetitive movements of speech and ritual. The following list is an extension of the magician's disciplinary techniques. They will be put into practice naturally as you follow this ritual's Willpower List:

✳ Honing the will through abstinence—*Day 1 o*n your Willpower List.

* Managing thoughts through creative visualization—*Day 2.*

* Feeding the soul through reading and a constant intake of knowledge—*Day 3.*

* Practical application of magic through the desire to help others and better yourself—*Day 4.*

* Daily self-examination to maintain stability and balance—*Day 5.*

Somewhere deep within us exists the expert marksman, the black belt in karate, the adept of the magical arts. Through the Dragonflame philosophy and by enforcing a Willpower List similar to the one just given in the proper manner, we are able to create the right amount of psychic pressure to awaken that part of our subconscious mind or magical self that already knows how to wield the sword of power. This part of us stays in a primordial sleep state until we find the proper knowledge to "kiss it awake," just as the prince did in the modernized version of the famous fairy tale *Snow White.*

First, the concept that this can even occur must be brought to your attention. Then, as it is assimilated by all parts of your being, and if you follow the Dragonflame philosophy long enough and correctly, you will tap into this hidden part of yourself. As this happens more and more you will automatically find stability. It is then your choice whether to maintain it or let it go.

Anger Is Captivity

One of my first experiences in controlling and manipulating power came to me in an astral experience, out of which came the inspiration for this ritual. I had been fighting with a decision regarding whether or not to fire an employee who was insubordinate. Letting someone go is always a difficult decision, and in my opinion should not be made quickly. But after my confrontation with this person I was very angry and found it difficult to remain impartial. In fact, I was so filled with anger that for a few days I could actually feel my stomach burning. I was making myself ill.

During this time I was not able to make any decisions or wield any magic. As I laid down to take an afternoon nap I kept going over the situation, becoming more and more upset. Then I heard a voice within me say, "Anger is captivity." It was like a light went on. Immediately, I started self-examination. It went something like this:

Why am I angry? I lost my cool because this particular employee had the audacity to lie so blatantly to me. I was unprepared.

There it was. The truth really did set me free. I visualized myself being liberated from captivity and experienced an emotional release. Soon after, I fell asleep and awakened on the astral realm. I heard myself chanting the spell contained in this ritual. Then I became aware that I had entered another scene. Here is the excerpt from my journal:

I was holding a sword in my right hand. It felt totally natural even though I have never taken fencing lessons. All of my actions happened automatically, without any premeditation. The next thing I knew I was fighting [the grumpy employee], who had a sword as well. I backed the enemy up a staircase and into a large closet. I felt at ease. All my movements were being made for me effortlessly as if a spirit had taken me over. All at once I flung my competitor's sword out of his hand and pressed the point of my sword at the center of his chest. I heard myself say, "Surrender!"

Suddenly I woke up.

The next day, before I could even say, "Pack up your stuff and leave," the employee started shouting at me. Obviously, guilt and anger had gotten the best of him. Like magic, I was completely calm and had the perfect response. My intellect and words were as sharp and powerful as the sword I used on the astral. I fired the person and moved on with my day, knowing that I made the correct decision. The now ex-employee left defeated, with the proverbial tail between his legs.

The end result of my experience and magic was personal transformation. A change in my character occurred, enabling me to handle the situation better. And, this change stuck. The interesting part is that I would never have thought of utilizing the energies of Geburah (the essence of power) to resolve my issues with an employee. It was unexpected, as are most things in magic.

As you go about working this ritual keep in mind that there is no way to intuit how it will manifest. Trust in the god Mars and expect the unexpected.

Willpower List

If you find some of the appointed tasks in this willpower list too daunting, you may substitute them with ones that are less challenging. Check the Appendix for extra help. Remember, what you put into the ritual is what you get out of it.

Day 1: Sacrifice

Give up something that you really enjoy for 24 hours, such as smoking, drinking coffee or soda, or watching TV. Be sure to assign a time to it. For example, *I choose to abstain from drinking coffee from 12 midnight to 11:59 p.m.*

Day 2: Visualize a white lemniscate (infinity sign)

Sit in front of a white candle. Relax yourself with some deep breathing, light the candle, and focus on the flame. Begin to look with your peripheral vision. This helps induce meditation and clear the mind. After 10 seconds or so, close your eyes and imagine a lemniscate made out of white fire. Hear the flames. See them pulsing with energy. Hold this image as long as you can. When other thoughts disturb you, do not become frustrated. Simply let them pass through your mind unobstructed. Become aware that they were superfluous and go back to the lemniscate. A good session will usually last around 10 minutes. Do this two times on the same day. For the second visualization imagine the lemniscate made out of red fire.

The lemniscate symbolizes pure spirit, where all power originates. Visualizing it strongly and long enough sends a pulse into the astral asking for power. Pondering its form will help you clear your mind and improve concentration. It is pure, directed energy. If successfully tapped into and directed, it will manifest your desire.

Thoughts to associate with the lemniscate are:

* Pure power removes all obstacles because there is nothing that can stand in its way.

* You no longer receive or give upset or negativity within its presence.

❋   All quibbling, arguments, and difficulties cease to exist within its presence.

❋   Simply becoming aware of its existence will help you align with it.

Day 3: Read sacred knowledge

Anything you can find, research, and assimilate about the Sephirah Geburah will help the potency of this ritual. Suggested reading: *The Witches Qabala* by Ellen Cannon Reed and *The Mystical Qabalah* by Dion Fortune.

Day 4: Practical application

Spend the day choosing and gathering supplies for another ritual from this book, which you will perform within six weeks of completing this ritual.

Day 5: Self-examination

At the end of the day, find a quiet place where you will not be disturbed. As well as you can, begin writing a list of everything you did from the moment you woke up. Some of your mundane actions may be grouped together (see the following sample).

Find the general tone of your day: was it boring, routine, mechanical, fun, exciting, frustrating? Just use a few words to describe it. Follow each question in the sample self-examination, and write down the answers in your magic journal.

At the end, you'll be asked to choose one or two segments from your day that you wish you had handled differently or would like to have changed. You will mentally project yourself back into the situations and visualize them happening the way you want—always with a positive energy and tone.

Get into a habit of doing this as often as possible or whenever a negative emotion arises. It will help you:

* Confront, define, and manage your emotions better

* Temper your anger and remove anxiety from future events

* Improve your confidence and memory

* Act as a stimulus for stability and balance

Remember, simple and pragmatic is what you're after. Do not feel that you need to write every detail or have a huge journal entry. Just the basics will do. The object is to force yourself to analyze your actions for the day and question how you spent your time. If you see *how* you react then you can change the *way* you react—especially if it is not yielding beneficial results the first time around. Ultimately, the analysis creates discipline and helps set up your future for success.

Here's a helpful hint before continuing. Throughout the day state the affirmation,

Now I choose to be aware of my every thought.

It is also helpful to give yourself triggers to help bring the affirmation to mind. For example, tell yourself that every time you cross your legs you will state the affirmation. Or every time you go up or down stairs you will say it. With continued practice this affirmation will help you become a master at observing your thoughts.

Sample Self-Examination

Daily Self-Examination
Saturday, November 15, 2011

Morning

Woke up feeling rested. Made some coffee and watched the morning news.

Had polite conversation with a friend.

Said daily affirmations as I made my bed, washed dishes, and prepared for the day.

Did some yoga. (Felt resistance to exercising/yoga. Had to push myself.)

Shaved, showered, did morning meditations. Felt a bit rushed (became aware of it, though, and focused on calming down).

Continued working on entry in my journal.

Morning Synopsis

How did you feel as the morning started?

Rested. Healthy.

Where were your thoughts mainly focused?

My thoughts were focused mainly on psychic development and knowledge as directed through my affirmations.

Were there morning challenges? Did you over-come them? If not, how could you overcome them in the future?

Resistance to exercise and a rushed, anxious feeling.

I was able to fight through the resistance to exercise. I forced myself to do yoga for about 10 minutes. Better than nothing. Felt better after I did it.

I worked through the anxiety by confronting it and asking myself why I felt it. The anxiety stemmed from the feeling that there wasn't enough time to accomplish everything I wanted. I told myself that I would finish what I could, and the rest would have to wait. There's ample time!

Tomorrow I will change my affirmations to relaxation and control.

Afternoon

Had some lunch. Not too healthy. Lots of protein and carbs. Need to watch my diet tomorrow to balance it out.

Began meditation in preparation for business meetings.

Meetings went well.

Afternoon Synopsis

How did you feel as the morning ended and afternoon started?

In a calm mood. Grounded.

Where were your thoughts mainly focused?

On helping my clients. On the spiritual and mundane.

Were there afternoon challenges? Did you overcome them? If not, how could you overcome them in the future?

No challenges. Proper amount of healthy stress to do a good job.

Evening

Had some dinner. Healthy snacks and vegetables.

Read about the god Pan and lit a red candle to him asking for help to raise my vibrational level.

Spent time reading and studying tarot with a friend.

Worked on creative writing and learning new vocabulary.

Ended the evening by taking a bath in Epsom salt and essential oil of neroli.

Evening Synopsis

How did you feel as the afternoon ended and evening started?

A little excited. Wasn't sure how to spend my time at first.

Where were your thoughts mainly focused?

On the spiritual and mundane. But overwhelmingly the spiritual. Perhaps unbalanced.

Were there evening challenges? Did you overcome them? If not, how could you overcome
them in the future?

I felt as the evening began that there was too much
spiritual and a lack of pleasure. So, I decided to
socialize with a friend and indulge in the Epsom salt/
neroli bath.

Overall Analysis

How did you feel as you went to bed?

Relaxed

What thoughts went through your mind as you
were drifting off to sleep?

I concentrated on asking Spirit what else I needed
to write about...concentrated on improving, editing
journal entries.

If you could change one thing about today, what
would it be? Write it out and imagine it unfolding
just as you would have liked it to.

I would have eaten less for lunch and exercised more
in the morning. I would have taken more time for
myself and less business meetings.

Now I choose to take only one or two appointments
per day. I imagine myself exercising 20 to 30 minutes in the morning and eating a healthy, well-balanced
lunch with vegetables, protein, and almost no
carbohydrates.

New affirmation: *Now I choose to radiate health and
beauty.*

<u>Fill in the Blanks</u>

My day was too spiritual.

My day was very calm.

My day was spent too much in one place. But also rewarding monetarily and very gratifying because I was able to help clients.

Altar Arrangements and Instructions

Dragonflame Talisman

Red Candle   White Candle

Cauldron with Florida Water

Oil Diffuser

* Place the Dragonflame talisman back and center of your altar if you choose not to wear it.

* Dress the red taper candle with ginger oil using the GPS system for this ritual. Place it on the back left corner of the altar (from the perspective of facing your altar).

* Dress the white taper candle with ginger oil using the same GPS system and place it on the back right corner of the altar, opposite the red candle.

❋   Place either your oil diffuser or incense on the front left corner. If you are using an oil diffuser, fill it with water and put five drops of ginger oil in it.

❋   Place your receptacle or cauldron in the center of the altar. Make sure you place it on something fireproof such as a stone or piece of ceramic tile. I use a natural piece of stone and also have a ceramic tile underneath it just to be safe.

❋   Pour about a quarter cup of the Hoyt's Cologne or Florida Water into the cauldron. Keep the Dragon's Blood resin close by; you will need it on the last day of the ritual.

Victory Spell

For each day of the ritual you will:

1.   Prepare your altar (follow altar arrangements).

2.   Put up a magic circle (optional, but recommended).

3.   Light the oil diffuser or incense.

4.   Light the white candle first.

5.   Light the red candle second.

6.   Enter a relaxed state.

7.   Ask Mars to guide you.

8.   Raise both arms so that they are parallel to the ground (hands straight out to the sides), with your palms down. Turn slowly three times counter-clockwise in one place as you chant the first part of the spell:

All obstacles removed momentum begun

As above, so below positivity spun

9. Standing in the same fashion, palms up, turn slowly
    three times clockwise in one place as you chant the
    second part of the spell:

    Health and power invoked great strength and full force

    As above, so below now shall follow due course

10. Light the Hoyt's Cologne or Florida Water and be-
    gin visualizing a red lemniscate in the flames of the
    cauldron. Put your hands up in benediction pose and
    pour energy into it as you chant the spell in its entirety
    again, this time without turning. Keep chanting the
    spell until the flames of the fire go out. You can con-
    tinue longer if you wish.

11. When you are finished chanting, release the image of
    the lemniscate by placing your hands underneath it
    and lifting it up to the god Mars. Imagine it being re-
    leased into his care, and put your left forefinger to your
    lips as if to say, "Shhhhh." This will stop the energy
    from coming back.

12. Release and thank the spirits and Mars.

13. Take down the magic circle if you have put one up.

14. Extinguish the candles in reverse (remember to use a
    candle snuffer).

15. On the last day of the ritual you will follow this list
    again. The only difference will be that you put the

Dragon's Blood resin into the cauldron with the Hoyt's Cologne or Florida Water. Then light it and start the visualization of the lemniscate. Everything else will remain the same.

Here's the spell in its entirety:

Victory Spell

All obstacles removed momentum begun

As above, so below positivity spun

Health and power invoked great strength and full force

As above, so below now shall follow due course

Enhancements for the Advanced Student

✳ Before you begin the spell, intone/vibrate *Elohim Gibor*, *Mars*, *Khamael*, *Seraphim*, *Graphiel*, *Bartzabel*, *Geburah*, and *Madim*.

HOLY NAME	EXPLANATION
Elohim Gibor	God Name
Mars	God/Goddess Name
Khamael	Archangel
Seraphim	Choir of Angels

Graphiel	Intelligence of the planet Mars
Bartzabel	Spirit of the planet Mars
Geburah	Sephirah (sacred emanation)
Madim	Mundane Chakra

* Time the start day of your ritual so the last day coincides with the full moon or lands on a Tuesday (the day of Mars).

* Perform the last day of the ritual during the planetary hour of Mars.

Lakshmi/Ganesha Ritual (For Monetary Growth)

Whatever you do, or dream you can, begin it. Boldness has genius and power and magic in it .

—Johann Wolfgang von Goethe

Goal: Monetary growth.

Purpose: So that I may weave my own destiny.

Sacrifice: Fear.

Sacrificing fear means to be courageous. Promise the goddess Lakshmi and the god Ganesha that you will be stronger in the face of adversity.

Supplies: Dragonflame talisman (can be worn or placed on altar), lotus oil (may be substituted with rose oil or rose incense), one purple candle, one purple vase, fresh tulips, mala beads (Buddhist prayer beads), statue of Ganesha and Lakshmi, pictures of goals (see below)

Duration: 4 days (The number 4 is associated with the planet Jupiter in the Practical Qabalah. It symbolizes wisdom, philosophy, expansion, money, and good luck.)

Offering: Burn Lotus oil, or a substitute, in an oil diffuser each day of the ritual to Lakshmi and Ganesha. It will also be used to bless the candle.

Fill out your Willpower List on your own for this ritual in your magic journal. (Check the Appendix for extra help and inspiration).

Mantra Means "Free Your Mind"

The power of mantra lies at the heart of this ritual, giving it a strong pulse. The word *mantra* stems from two Sanskrit words: *Manas*, or "mind," and *Trai*, a root word meaning "grants liberation." Put them together and you get "free your mind."

A mantra is a word, syllable, or phrase, usually in Sanskrit, that holds a particular energetic essence and meaning. By repeating or chanting the mantra it frees the mind of extraneous thoughts and aligns you with its own force. A set of 108 beads, called mala beads, is used to help make the chanting easier. *Mala*, which means "garlands" in Sanskrit, work like Catholic rosary beads. Each bead equals one mantra. This way, your mind does not have to keep count and the mantra can do its job more easily and bring you into a trance state.

In this ritual, the object is to chant the mantra using one entire repetition of the mala prayer beads to help you enter an altered state and tap into the mantra's energy. For our purposes a traditional 108-bead mala is fine. While I was working this ritual I was able to go into a deep meditative state while chanting the Lakshmi/Ganesha mantra, and I had a psychic vision. I saw and felt myself sitting in a huge monolithic throne like a raja or Indian king. The vision only lasted a second or two, but it was long enough to fill me with an intense sense of power and knowing. I knew that it was not something I imagined because it was completely unexpected. I also knew at that moment that the ritual had worked. The vision affirmed itself by manifesting on the earth realm several months later with a windfall of great luck.

Work hard at your rituals until you have a psychic experience, lucid dream, or vision. Make it a goal to strive for some type of spiritual affirmation. When it happens it means that your ritual or spell has worked on an astral level ("as above") and therefore must manifest on the earth plane in some shape or form (so below). If this does not happen quickly, be patient and gentle with yourself. It will come in time. Remember, practice makes perfect.

As a side note, for those of you who are just starting and unfamiliar with the Qabalistic associations under *Enhancements for the Advanced Student*, your magic is still very potent. Without the Qabalistic enhancements you are working more from the instincts than the mind. This is called low magic. Low magic tends to work more quickly than high magic, but will taper off faster. High magic, using more of your cerebral aspect and the Qabalistic enhancements, takes longer to peak, but its effects will last longer. Either way, when magic works it grants you a window of opportunity. Grab it and run with it. It is up to you to make it last!

Hindu God Ganesha: Destroyer of Obstacles

Sometimes unknown obstacles are stopping us from reaching our goals. In the Hindu pantheon the god Ganesha, famously depicted with the head of an elephant, is evoked first to remove them. The power behind his name is so great that it only needs to be uttered once to get its full affect. Believe that statement when you perform this ritual, and when it works, you will know it to be true. This is how you can remove barriers of doubt within yourself.

Each time one of your magical endeavors is successful a layer of doubt is peeled away that was formerly restricting communication between your conscious and subconscious mind. The more magic you practice, the more successes you will have, the more layers will be removed, the more your subconscious mind will accept the reality of magic, and the easier magic will become for you.

If you continue in this fashion, the next time you need to remove an obstacle all you will need to do is bless a black candle with some uncrossing oil, light it, and say the word *Ganesha*. Because your subconscious mind knows that it has worked in the past (not believes—*knows*) its pool of energy will be readily accessible in the present.

This is a compounding effect that takes a long time for most people to achieve, so be patient with yourself. Also, this is a simplified explanation for something that can only be understood through personal experience and application. It cannot be rushed, but achieved only through much work and dedication. Now, before you become totally discouraged, here are some words of comfort: If I could do it, you can do it!

Hindu Goddess Lakshmi: Bringer of Prosperity

After Ganesha has removed the obstacles, the profound, abundant energy of Lakshmi may flow freely into your core. The Hindu goddess of beauty and wealth, Lakshmi appeared to me in a lucid dream as an elegant older woman dressed in fine clothing. Her energy felt wise, comforting, and like that of a grand matriarch.

This vision came to me at a time when I really wanted to change my life situation but did not know how to go about it. I was feeling frustrated and a bit defeated. When I saw Lakshmi, I immediately knelt down before her. She put her hand on my head and never spoke. But as her energy flowed into my subtle body it conveyed a meaning. It was as if she were saying, "It will be alright, child, just let go and trust me. Don't fret. Be strong, child." I remember waking up and wanting to burst into tears of relief. If you want to understand her energy, that is what you should think of—someone whose inner self is so wealthy and beautiful that simply being in its presence banishes all despair and fills you with hope.

Pictures of Goals

You have the whole of creation, the entire cosmos at your disposal. What will you make of it? This is the mindset you need at the start of this ritual. What you think is what you will ultimately manifest. If you have a clear image of this thought (or thoughts), then it will manifest more easily. Sometimes it is a challenge figuring out what these thoughts are, let alone focusing on them. That's why magazines, the Internet, and anything that has images already created for us will come in handy for this portion of the ritual. Enjoy yourself, and take your time as you go through any type of media that may have a picture of what it is you desire or that represents monetary growth to you. Cut the images out, print them out, or draw them. Whatever the case, get as many or as few as you like to use in this ritual.

At first, you may want to choose any images that strike your fancy and then weed through them later. Some of the images will be goals that you want to achieve; others will simply be inspirational. It does not matter; they both serve the same purpose. But the space on your altar is limited, so boil it down to the most potent ones.

For monetary growth to occur you have to feel abundant. Ask yourself the question, "What makes me feel abundant and rich?" and start looking through magazines. Whatever pictures you come across that arouse that emotion are the ones you want.

The goal of the pictures is to:

* Stimulate the emotions
* Create motivation and inspiration
* Focus your thoughts on monetary growth
* Create an image of your goal on the astral realm

The pictures are more tools of mental and emotional stimulation than anything else, so do not limit yourself to images of diamond bracelets and expensive cars. You might want to use a tarot card such as the Magician, representing the fact that you make your own good luck or destiny. Or, perhaps you may want to use a picture of the sun, representing fame, happiness, and health. The sky's the limit. Have fun and choose with your heart, not with your head. Here's an affirmation to say while you are perusing different magazines or the Internet:

Now I choose to use all of the cosmos to achieve my goals.

Altar Arrangements and Instructions

✳ Place fresh-cut tulips at the back center of the altar.

✳ Put pictures of goals on the left and right sides of the altar.

✳ Place the oil diffuser at the upper left, and Mala beads at the upper right.

✳ The statues of Ganesha and Lakshmi should be front and center.

✳ The Dragonflame talisman goes in front of Ganesha and Laskhmi if you choose not to wear it.

✳ Place a purple candle in a purple vase in the center of your altar.

	Fresh-Cut Tulips	
Pics of Goals	Purple Candle in Purple Vase	Pics of Goals
	Ganesha and Lakshmi	
	Dragonflame Talisman	
Oil Diffuser		Mala Beads

Ganesha Spell

1. Prepare your altar.

2. Put up a magic circle (optional, but recommended).

3. Advanced practitioners may perform the Lesser Banishing Ritual of the Pentagram and/or the Banishing Ritual of the Hexagram. (If you do not know either,

don't worry; it is not necessary to make the ritual work.)

4. Light the offering.

5. Light the purple candle.

6. Enter a relaxed state.

7. Say the spell once.
   Ganesha, may the color of this candle please you. With great power, kind spirits, fly to wherever you must to make my money grow and grow and grow! With harm to none and for the greatest good of all. So be it! Thank you in advance.

8. Sit in lotus position in front of your altar. Focus on the flame of the candle and try to empty your mind of thoughts.

9. Begin chanting the mantra for one entire round on the mala beads. While chanting, visualize all your goals manifesting.
   Om Gum Shrim Maha Lakshmiyei Swaha
   Ohm - Gum - Shrim - Maha - Lock - shmee - yea – Swaha
   Translation: *Let all obstacles to my abundance be removed and let the flow of the energy of abundance be released within me.*

10. Release and thank God Ganesha and Goddess Lakshmi and the spirits.

11. If you opened with the LBRP and/or BRH, repeat them here to close harmoniously.

12. Take down the magic circle if you have put one up. Also, if you used the LBRP/BRH to open and close, that means you have put up four magic circles and therefore must take down, or reabsorb, four magic circles.

13. Extinguish the candle (remember to use a candle snuffer).

Enhancements for the Advanced Student

✸ Before you begin the ritual, intone/vibrate *El*, *Ganesha*, *Lakshmi*, *Tzadkiel*, *Chasmalim*, *Hismael*, *Iophiel*, *Chesed*, and *Tzedek*.

HOLY NAMES	EXPLANATION
El	God Name
Ganesha	Name of Hindu God
Lakshmi	Name of Hindu Goddess
Tzadkiel	Archangel
Chasmalim	Choir of Angels
Hismael	Intelligence of Jupiter
Iophiel	Spirit of Jupiter
Chesed	Sephirah (sacred emanation)
Tzedek	Mundane Chakra

✸ Perform on a full moon or when the moon is in Cancer.

✸ Perform on a Thursday at sunrise or in the planetary hour of Jupiter.

If you have completed any one of the rituals found in this book, congratulations! You have focused and directed a lot of energy not only toward your goal but also toward your destiny and spiritual evolution. And now, some quality advice: release and wait in patient receptivity.

Waiting for your wish to manifest will cause unnecessary anxiety. Instead, feel secure knowing that the force of your will directed through the Dragonflame philosophy is manifesting your desire even as you read this sentence.

You create your life. Anything that comes quickly, however, also tends to leave quickly. Allow your wish to manifest at the most beneficial time—even if it takes a decade—and it will be long-lasting. Dragonflame, the universe, and your True Will are working in conjunction to ensure you are the right person, in the right place, at the right time.

As you allow Dragonflame's philosophy to guide your magic and spirituality, something wonderful happens. You will notice a new rhythm in your life. By completing one ritual and choosing to perform another, you have automatically generated a unique cycle. You have participated in beginning a particular ritual, the ending or the releasing of it, and, eventually, waiting however long it takes before beginning or choosing another.

A quotation by the spiritual philosopher Deepak Chopra summarizes the concept of ritual patterns and maintaining smooth transitions within your cycle: *When you live your life with an appreciation of coincidences and their meanings, you connect with the underlying field of infinite possibilities.*

Let this insight work alongside Dragonflame's magical philosophy. Look for synchronicities and Divine omens for guidance in choosing your next ritual, creating your next life experience, and furthering your spiritual evolution.

Fruit-Bearing Tree

CONCLUSION

Creation is our birthright, along with its twin, Free Will. Creation and Free Will are constantly moving, hand in hand, like children traveling along a path full of impulses and inspirations. One desires; one acts. At first they are unaware of the consequences but then are forced to learn through trial and error. Showing them a better way to achieve results, Experience quickly becomes their teacher. In time, the twins learn from mistakes and are able to make more sophisticated choices. Evolving along with Nature, gaining acuity of mind, they begin to mature and look beyond the superficial. Concepts such as interconnectedness and cause and effect are taken into consideration as the twins have gained yet another teacher: Wisdom. Now, able to control powerful energies, the twins have transformed into adept magicians. They are at this point in time superior artistic beings able to enjoy and share the fruits of their creative labor. And so it goes. With the tools of and respect for Creation, Free Will, Experience, and Wisdom, you too can stroll along this path of transformation. Such is the nature of Dragonflame!

It is my hope that this book has imparted simple yet radical means for you to simultaneously work magic, learn more about yourself, and grow in sacred wisdom. You can manifest whatever you desire! Most importantly, however, you will transform spiritually in the process. Enjoy Dragonflame's Magical GPS system and use it often. Allow its philosophy and power to teach you to become bold and to change your life on a grand scale. Finally, as I have oftentimes repeated, follow the golden rule: harm none and wish others well, as I wish you the same.

GLOSSARY

alchemy: A philosophy and form of chemistry sharing the purpose of finding the Philosopher's Stone and transmuting base metals into gold. As a philosophy, it is the metaphorical process of transforming the base nature of the human soul into spiritual enlightenment.

alpha state: One of four brainwave categories (in order of frequency, from most alert to deep sleep, they are beta, alpha, theta, and delta). This state is considered one of relaxed awareness, and it allows the subconscious mind to be more receptive to affirmations, mental imagery, and visualizations.

astral body: The nonphysical body, connected to or coexisting with our physical body, vibrating at the same frequency as the astral realm. It is the vehicle our consciousness uses to travel the astral realm. The astral body is also referred to as the subtle body, or subtle bodies.

astral realm: A nonphysical state of being, which vibrates at a higher frequency than the earth realm and our physical bodies. Known as the "astral" for short, it is the blueprint for all matter before it manifests on the earth plane. Also referred to as the "ethers" or the astral plane, it is associated with the Sephirah Yesod in the Qabalah.

BRH: Acronym for Banishing Ritual of the Hexagram. It is a ceremonial ritual originating from the mystery school known as the Golden Dawn. Using a system of geometric shapes and god names, the ritual creates a neutral environment for the magician to work in by removing all energy that may obstruct the magician from obtaining his/her goal.

chakra: Meaning "wheel" in Sanskrit, a chakra is a connection point between the physical body and the spiritual realm. A chakra is also one of many energy centers found on the body. Typically, there are seven primary chakras: crown, third eye, throat, heart, solar plexus, sacral, and root.

chi: Chinese word for universal life force and/or energy found in all living things (pronounced *chee*).

collective unconscious: A term coined by Swiss psychologist Carl Jung that defines the part of the unconscious mind that contains inherited, pre-existing forms (archetypes) common to all humanity.

ethers: *see* astral realm.

Great Work: The name of the spiritual path the alchemist embarks on in order to reach enlightenment and find the Philosopher's Stone. In alchemy, it is also referred to in Latin as the *Magnum Opus*.

Green Man: An image of a face surrounded by leaves and vegetation, used as a symbol of rebirth and the active, regenerative qualities found in Nature. The image is also known as the Horned God, or God of Wicca.

grimoire: Derived from the French word *grammaire*, meaning "grammar," it refers to any book of magic or spells, especially of a medieval time period.

Hermetic axiom(s): Seven principles attributed to Hermes Trismegistus, "Thrice-Great Hermes" (a representation of the mixture of the Greek God Hermes and the Egyptian God Thoth): mentalism, correspondence, vibration, polarity, rhythm, cause and effect, and gender. They are considered the backbone of Hermetic philosophy.

Higher Self: The Divine aspect within us that is closest to Creator and mediates between our spiritual self and lower self, or personality. According to the Practical Qabalah, the Higher Self, or True Self, resides in the Sephirah Tiphareth and is also known as the Holy Guardian Angel.

karma: An ancient Indian concept explaining the cycle of energy's cause and effect. The philosophy somewhat follows an energetic code found in magic, especially Wicca: what you do to others will come back three times to you.

kundalini: Translates as "coiled" from the Sanskrit. It is the life force or energy located at the base of the spine, coiled like a serpent. Through specialized meditation and yoga, this energy can be stimulated to rise upward along the spine, piercing through the seven primary chakras, resulting in psychic evolution.

LBRP: Acronym for Lesser Banishing Ritual of the Pentagram. It is a ceremonial ritual originating from the mystery school known as the Golden Dawn. Using a system of geometric shapes (earth-banishing pentagrams) and god names, the ritual creates a neutral environment for the magician to work in by removing all negative energy that may obstruct the magician from obtaining his/her goal.

lucid dream: A dream in which you are an active participant in the dreamscape and are able to manipulate the dream environment.

macrocosmic: A large perspective or representation of something smaller, usually of similar structure. For example, when speaking in philosophical and/or esoteric terminology, the universe (macrocosm) that we live in is a reflection of our inner universe (microcosm).

magic circle: A circle that you draw around yourself before performing a ritual. The circle can be imaginary (of white light, fire, etc.), physical (of string, salt, water, etc.), or both. Traditionally, it is used to cleanse your working space of unwanted energies, to define a boundary line of protection, and to create a focal point or center from which to work.

magical name or motto: A special name or phrase chosen by the practitioner to differentiate the aspect of the personality that practices magic (magical self) from the daily, mundane self.

mercury (alchemical): One of three philosophical concepts (mercury, salt, sulfur) referred to in the art of alchemy, not to be confused with the chemical mercury, or quicksilver.

microcosmic: A small perspective or representation of something greater, usually of similar structure. For example, when speaking in philosophical and/or esoteric terminology, our inner universe (microcosm) is a reflection of the outer universe (macrocosm) in which we live.

Philosopher's Stone: A magical elixir able to turn lead into gold and bestow immortality. In the occult, it is a metaphorical term describing the achievement of the Great Work or the attainment of spiritual enlightenment.

psyche: The mind, both conscious and unconscious, as well as the intuition, feeling, instinct, and sense of self.

salt (alchemical): One of three philosophical concepts (mercury, salt, sulfur) referred to in the art of alchemy, not to be confused with common table salt.

Sephiroth (*sing.:* **Sephirah**): A Hebrew word meaning "spheres" or "emanations," referring to 10 divine emanations or energies within the Qabalastic Tree of Life representing 10 different stages of the creation of the universe on a macrocosmic and microcosmic level.

subtle body: *see* astral body.

sulfur (alchemical): One of three philosophical concepts (mercury, salt, sulfur) referred to in the art of alchemy, not to be confused with the element sulfur.

talisman: Any object charged or imbued with a magician's will toward obtaining a particular goal.

tattwa: A representation of the essence of the five elements in Hindu philosophy. Each tattwa has been assigned a multitude of magical associations, among them a geometric shape and color: tejas/red triangle/fire, apas/silver crescent/water, vayu/blue sphere/air, prithivi/yellow rectangle or square/earth, akasha/egg shape/spirit.

totem: Any physical object or animal found in nature that has a special significance to you. There is no limit to the objects/animals that can be used as totems, and they can range from mineral, stone, flower, and herb to insect, bird, mammal, and beyond. Mythological creatures also apply, such as unicorns, griffins, satyrs, and the like. As long as it holds a personal interest or resonates with your life in some way, then it counts as a totem.

Tree of Life: A glyph or symbol, used in the Qabalah, consisting of 10 spheres or divine emanations believed to be a blueprint of the universe, both macrocosmic and microcosmic.

Triple Goddess: An esoteric archetype, prominent in Wicca and paganism/neo-paganism, representing the three cycles of the moon: new, full, and dark (which mirror the stages of a woman's life: maiden, mother, and crone). The Triple Goddess can also refer to the three destinies or fates, as well as ancient Greek goddess Hecate.

True Will: Working in accordance with your true destiny; being in harmony with Nature and Creator's divine plan. This term was defined by 20th-century magician Aleister Crowley.

vibrating (god names/power names): The process of intoning sacred names, god names, and words by elongating each of their syllables in a long, forceful tone, either mentally or out loud. The tone should "vibrate" through your body while you imagine it traveling or "vibrating" through the entirety of the universe, surpassing time itself.

willpower list: A list (or a singular item for the duration of one day and/or night) of sacrifices chosen by the practitioner for each day and/or night of a ritual, or any magical working. The energy created by the willpower list is directed toward a chosen deity, force, or entity ruling the magical work. It can also be directed to the Higher Self or any aspect of the personality in order to exercise the will and add energy to the magical working.

WILLPOWER LIST IDEAS

1. Expand your vocabulary. Learn a new vocabulary word and use it in a sentence throughout the day.

2. Make a special card for someone.

3. Bring flowers to someone.

4. Go to the gym or exercise.

5. Abstain from eating rich food.

6. Fast for one or more days.

7. Reorganize a room.

8. Don't watch TV for 24 hours.

9. Give a stranger a compliment.

10. Don't use text messaging for 24 hours.

11. Refrain from gossip and negative thinking for 24 hours.

12. Light a candle in remembrance of a loved one who has passed away.

13. Research something new.

14. Take a walk with a friend.

15. Drink only tea for a day or more (try to choose a tea that magically corresponds with your ritual. For example, drink chamomile tea if you are working with Tiphareth or the sun, Lavender if you are working with Hod or the planet Mercury, and so on).

16. Light a candle to a God/Goddess at the stroke of midnight—three nights in a row.

17. State your petition on your knees at the stroke of midnight—three nights in a row.

18. Go out of your way to do something nice for someone.

19. Volunteer at a local organization.

20. Abstain from sexual activity for a designated time.

21. Pack your own lunch for work for three consecutive, days.

22. Do three good deeds for the day.

23. Define your mental limitations. Write a list of what you think that means. Then, post it on your refrigerator and challenge yourself to overcome them. Each time you look at them, say this affirmation: *Now I choose to overcome my mental limitations.*

24. Make a list of good and bad opportunities that are in your present realm of being. Cross off the bad opportunities and vow not to look back. Choose one of the good opportunities and visualize it as if it's happening right now.

25. Practice yoga or qui gung at sunrise.

26. Spend time with the elderly.

REFERENCES AND RECOMMENDED READING

I suggest the following books for further research and to deepen your understanding of magic, totems, the Practical Qabalah, and philosophy in general. I found them to be inspirational and informative.

Andrews, Ted. *Animal-Wise: The Spirit Language and Signs of Nature*. Jackson, Tenn.: Dragonhawk, 1999.

Beyerl, Paul. *A Compendium of Herbal Magick*. Blaine, Wash.: Phoenix, 1998.

Carnie, L. V. *Chi Gung: Chinese Healing, Energy, and Natural Magick*. Woodbury, Minn.: Llewellyn, 2007.

Cicero, Chic, and Sandra Cicero. *Self-Initiation into the Golden Dawn Tradition*. Woodbury, Minn.: Llewellyn, 2003.

———. *Tarot Talismans: Invoke the Angels of Tarot*. Woodbury, Minn.: Llewellyn, 2006.

Fortune, Dion. *The Mystical Qabalah*. San Francisco: Weiser, 2000.

Gardiner, Philip. *Gnosis: The Secret of Solomon's Temple Revealed*. Franklin Lakes, N.J.: New Page Books, 2006.

Hopcke, Robert H. *A Guided Tour of the Collected Works of C.G. Jung*. Boston: Shambhala, 1999.

Kraig, Donald Michael. *Modern Magick: Twelve Lessons in the High Magickal Arts*. Woodbury, Minn.: Llewellyn, 2010.

Levi, Eliphas. *Transcendental Magic*. San Francisco: Weiser, 2001.

Reed, Ellen Cannon. *The Witches Qabala*. San Francisco: Weiser, 1997.

Regardie, Israel. *A Garden of Pomegranates*. Woodbury, Minn.: Llewellyn, 2002.

———. *The Golden Dawn*. Woodbury, Minn.: Llewellyn, 1993.

———. *The Tree of Life*. San Francisco: Weiser, 1995.

Three Initiates. *The Kybalion: The Hermetic Philosophy of Ancient Egypt and Greece*. 1912 reprint, Rough Draft Printing, 2012.

Tolle, Eckhart. *Practicing the Power of Now: Essential Teachings, Meditations, and Exercises from the Power of Now*. Novato, Calif.: New World Library, 2004.

Wang, Robert. *The Qabalistic Tarot*. San Francisco: Weiser, 1987.

INDEX

ABOUT THE AUTHOR

Lawren Leo attended Lynn University and Pepperdine University. Since then he has traveled throughout the United States, Great Britain, Western Europe, North Africa, and the Middle East studying esoteric philosophy, magical arts, and alternative religion, and giving readings. He has been practicing Wicca and High Magick and studying Qabalah for nearly three decades. Presently, he owns a metaphysical boutique called New Moon Books, Crystals & Candles, Inc., in Pompano Beach, Florida, where he also resides. He is also contributing author and editor to the electronic magazine *The Familiar*. Visit Newmoonbooks.org.